Fish amulet
hair pendants

DK EYEWITNESS BOOKS

ANCIENT EGYPT

Written by
GEORGE HART

Gold plaque
showing
pharaoh and
sun god Atum

Floral inlays
and molds

Bracelet with
lapis lazuli scarab
set in gold

DK
Dorling Kindersley

Paddle doll

Earrings

Wooden
cosmetic
spoon

DK

Dorling Kindersley

LONDON, NEW YORK, AUCKLAND, DELHI, JOHANNESBURG, MUNICH, PARIS and SYDNEY

For a full catalog, visit

DK www.dk.com

Project editor Phil Wilkinson
Designer Thomas Keenes
Senior editor Sophie Mitchell
Senior art editor Julia Harris
Editorial director Sue Unstead
Art director Anne-Marie Bulat
Special photography Peter Hayman
of the Department of Egyptian Antiquities,
British Museum

This Eyewitness ® Book has been conceived by
Dorling Kindersley Limited and Editions Gallimard

© 1990 Dorling Kindersley Limited
This edition © 2000 Dorling Kindersley Limited
First American edition, 1990

Published in the United States by
Dorling Kindersley Publishing, Inc.
375 Hudson Street,
New York, New York 10014

6 8 10 9 7

Dorling Kindersley books are available at special discounts for bulk
purchases for sales promotions or premiums. Special editions,
including personalized covers, excerpts of existing guides, and
corporate imprints can be created in large quantities for specific needs.
For more information, contact Special Markets Dept., Dorling Kindersley
Publishing, Inc., 95 Madison Ave., New York,
NY 10016; Fax: (800) 600-9098

Library of Congress Cataloging-in-Publication Data
Hart, George.
Ancient Egypt / written by George Hart;
photographs by Peter Hayman.
p. cm. — (Eyewitness Books)
Summary: A photo essay on ancient Egypt and
the people who lived there, documented through
the mummies, pottery, weapons, and other objects
they left behind. Describes their society, religion,
obsession with the afterlife, and methods of
mummification.
1. Egypt—Civilization—To 332 B.C.—Juvenile
literature. [1. Egypt—Civilization—To 332 B.C.]
I. Hayman, Peter, ill. II. Title.
DT61.H284 2000 932'.01—dc20 90-4106
ISBN 0-7894-5785-7 (pb)
ISBN 0-7894-5784-9 (hc)

Glass ear studs

Glass tube
for eye
paint

Color reproduction by Colourscan, Singapore
Printed in China by Toppan Printing Co. (Shenzhen) Ltd.

Pendant of lapis
lazuli bull's head
set in gold

DORLING KINDERSLEY 📖 EYEWITNESS BOOKS

ANCIENT EGYPT

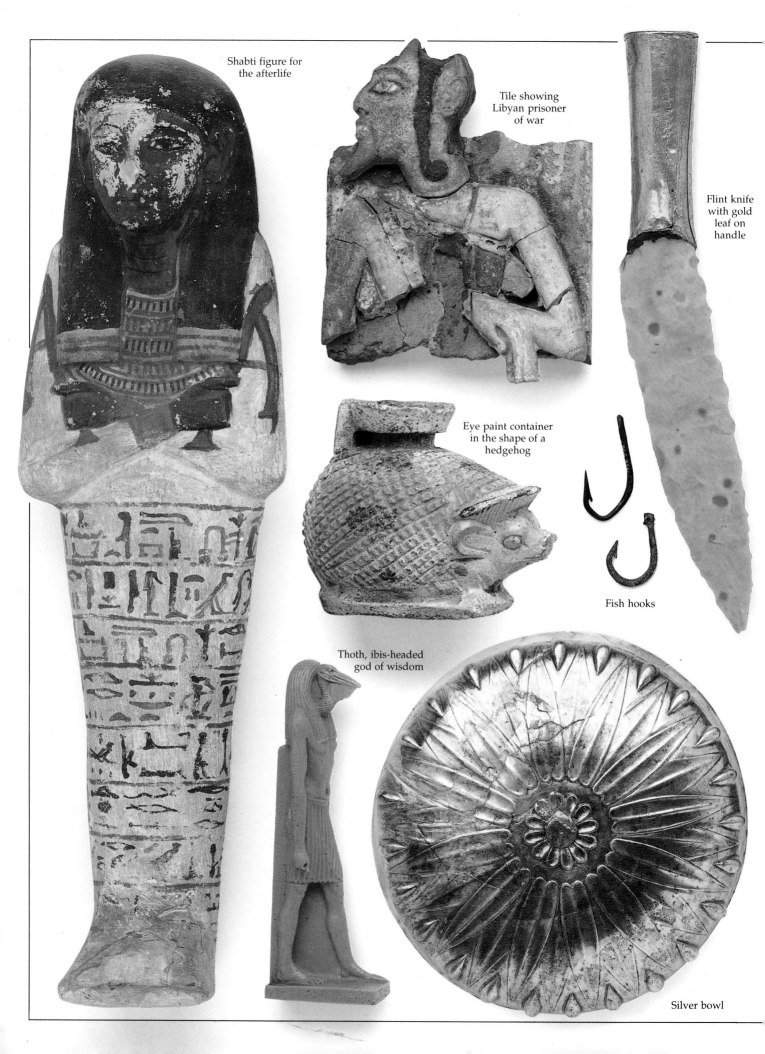

Shabti figure for the afterlife

Tile showing Libyan prisoner of war

Flint knife with gold leaf on handle

Eye paint container in the shape of a hedgehog

Fish hooks

Thoth, ibis-headed god of wisdom

Silver bowl

Contents

Sketch on flake of limestone

Egypt before the pharaohs

THE PERIOD we usually think of as ancient Egypt is the time when Egypt was ruled by the pharaohs - after c. 3000 B.C. But who lived in Egypt before the pharaohs? In the early Stone Age people in Egypt lived in areas fairly high above sea level near the Nile from the Delta to Aswan. Beginning in about 5000 B.C., settlers came to Egypt from Palestine and Syria, from the Libyan tribes living to the west, and from Nubia in the south. Shortly before 3000 B.C., traders from southern Iraq also sailed to Egypt, and some, attracted by the fertility of the country, stayed on. Soon these early settlers began to grow barley and to domesticate cattle, and to build villages of mud huts in parts of the flood plain that seemed safe from the annual Nile flood. Slate palettes and elaborately carved ivory objects, as well as fine pots, often buried with their owners in brick-lined graves, have been found dating from the period before 3000 B.C.

MACE HEAD
The mace was the kind of weapon used to give the death blow to a wounded enemy. But the smooth surfaces and superb carving of this example mean it was probably carried by a ruler or high commander on ceremonial occasions.

COMB AND CONCUBINE
The African elephant and hippopotamus provided early craftsmen with plenty of ivory. The comb handle is carved into the shape of a gazelle, perhaps because its owner enjoyed hunting this creature. The female figure was placed in a tomb and was meant to provide the owner with a female companion in the afterlife.

ANCIENT BODY
Before mummification evolved, burials involved arranging the corpse in a "sleeping" position with the elbows and knees drawn together. The body was placed in a pit with a selection of possessions, and sand was thrown on top of it. The sand absorbed all the water from the body, drying it out and preserving it, so the person's spirit would recognize it and inhabit it. Here you can see the fairly well preserved hair and features of a man who died about 5,000 years ago. When he was found, some people thought that he was still lifelike enough to warrant a nickname – Ginger, because of his red hair.

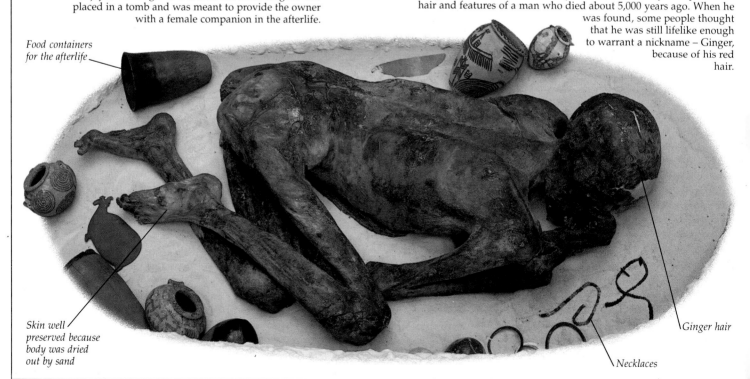

Food containers for the afterlife

Skin well preserved because body was dried out by sand

Ginger hair

Necklaces

STONE VASE
This vase was carved with simple flint or copper tools from a mottled stone called breccia. Quartz was used for polishing the surface.

Carnelian

Feldspar

NECKLACES
Early jewelers used semiprecious stones from the deserts. Favorites were feldspar (green) and carnelian (orange). Luxury items like these necklaces show us that even before the pharaohs not every laborer was used to till the soil or hunt for food – craftsmen were already valued members of society and were well rewarded for their skills.

Smooth shape made by simple tools

Eye inlaid with ivory

POTTERY VASE
Nile silt and clay from the edges of the flood plain provided materials for the early potters. This pot's tapering base was designed to fit in a stand or to rest in a depression in the ground. The circular spirals are meant to give the impression of a vessel carved from stone.

Spiral design

COSMETIC PALETTE
Some of the oldest surviving Egyptian objects are slate palettes. Some are rectangular; others are carved in animal shapes like hippos, turtles, falcons, or this obese ram. The surface was used for grinding minerals for eye paint (p. 58).

On the banks of the Nile

THE DESERT, also called the Red Land, covers more than 90 percent of Egypt. The desert supported only small settlements in wadis (river valleys) and oases. The Egyptians lived on the banks of the Nile River or beside canals extending from it. The area near the Nile was Kemet, or the Black Land, named after the rich dark silt on which the farmers grew their crops. Without this fertility, there would have been no civilization in Egypt. From ancient times right up to today the pattern of life in Egypt for the majority of the population has depended on the exploitation of its fertile agricultural resources. The Nile flood began the year for the Egyptian farmer, when the river, rising from the swelling waters of the Blue Nile and White Nile, which converge just north of Khartoum in the Sudan, brought deposits of silt into Egypt. When the Nile waters subsided, the farmers went to work sowing barley and emmer wheat. The result usually was a good summer harvest.

FAMINE
In a climate of extremes, crops could sometimes fail and famine could hit the population hard. Statues of people like this beggar remind us of this problem in ancient Egypt.

A RIVERSIDE PEOPLE
The ancient Egyptians lived in a strip of land on either side of the Nile, where the Nile flood made the land fertile. The flood area is shown in green on this map.

Nile Delta

Nile River

Red Sea

Desert

Herdsman driving cattle with a stick

Scribe with his palette

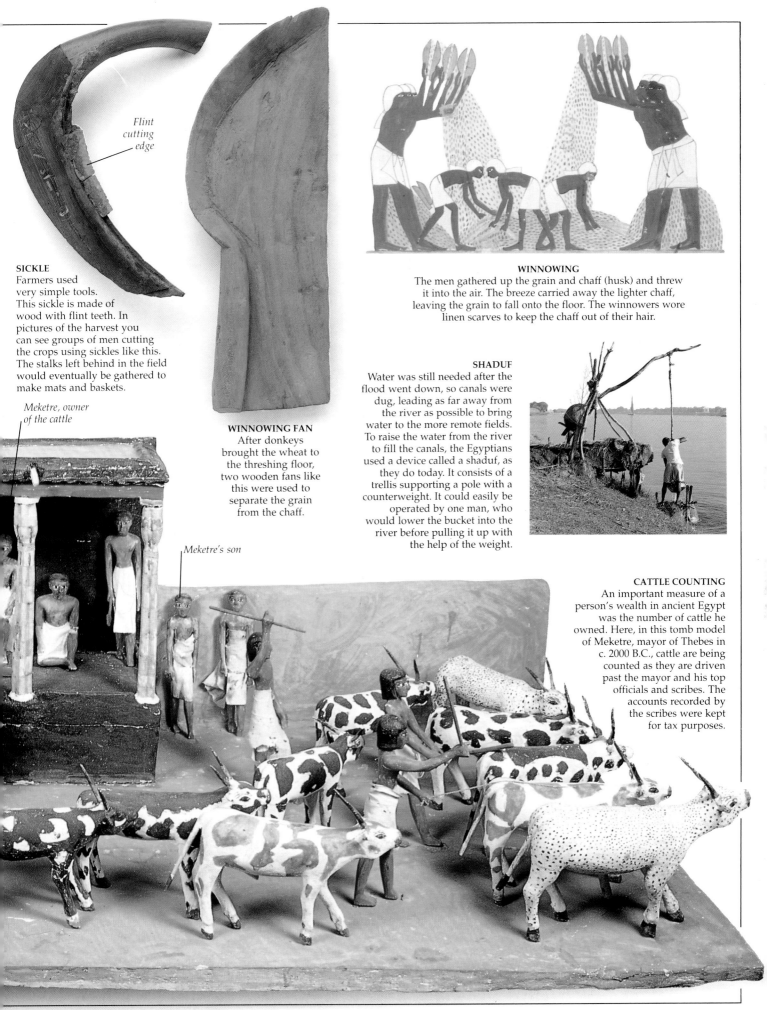

SICKLE
Farmers used very simple tools. This sickle is made of wood with flint teeth. In pictures of the harvest you can see groups of men cutting the crops using sickles like this. The stalks left behind in the field would eventually be gathered to make mats and baskets.

Flint cutting edge

Meketre, owner of the cattle

Meketre's son

WINNOWING FAN
After donkeys brought the wheat to the threshing floor, two wooden fans like this were used to separate the grain from the chaff.

WINNOWING
The men gathered up the grain and chaff (husk) and threw it into the air. The breeze carried away the lighter chaff, leaving the grain to fall onto the floor. The winnowers wore linen scarves to keep the chaff out of their hair.

SHADUF
Water was still needed after the flood went down, so canals were dug, leading as far away from the river as possible to bring water to the more remote fields. To raise the water from the river to fill the canals, the Egyptians used a device called a shaduf, as they do today. It consists of a trellis supporting a pole with a counterweight. It could easily be operated by one man, who would lower the bucket into the river before pulling it up with the help of the weight.

CATTLE COUNTING
An important measure of a person's wealth in ancient Egypt was the number of cattle he owned. Here, in this tomb model of Meketre, mayor of Thebes in c. 2000 B.C., cattle are being counted as they are driven past the mayor and his top officials and scribes. The accounts recorded by the scribes were kept for tax purposes.

Famous pharaohs

The oval enclosing the hieroglyphs that make up a royal name is called a cartouche. This one contains the name of King Tuthmosis III.

T HE KING was not only the most powerful and important man in Egypt – he was thought to be a god. He was known as the pharaoh – a word which derives from a respectful way of referring to the king by describing him as the "great house" (*per-ao*), meaning the palace where he lived. The Queen of Egypt was also thought of as a goddess but was usually given the title of "Great Royal Wife" – only rarely did women rule Egypt in their own right. There was an effective system of teaching a prince to become a pharaoh, which included training him to be an expert sportsman and potential war leader. Often the ruling pharaoh would adopt his heir as co-regent to enable a smooth takeover when the king died. Sometimes princes had to wait a long time. One pharaoh, Pepy II, holds the record for the longest reign of any monarch. Pepy II came to the throne when he was six years old. He was still king of Egypt 94 years later when he was 100. It is remarkable that in Egypt's long history there are only a few references to pharaohs being assassinated, usually as a result of a plot in the court to put a prince who was not the true heir onto the throne.

ARMLESS QUEEN
This statue of an Egyptian queen is from around 700 B.C. Her arms were attached separately but have been lost, as has her crown of plumes.

Osiris, God of the underworld

Akhenaten

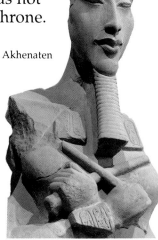

HATSHEPSUT
This determined woman ruled Egypt for about 20 years. She was supposed to be regent for her young stepson, but took over the reins of government. She wore the pharaoh's crown and royal ceremonial beard. In this sculpture she wears the crown of Upper Egypt, which bears the cobra goddess.

Nefertiti

AKHENATEN AND NEFERTITI
In Akhenaten's reign the traditional Egyptian gods were banished – only the sun god was worshiped. To break the links with other gods, Akhenaten founded a new capital city and closed the temples of other gods. Queen Nefertiti helped her husband set up the cult of the sun god Aten and probably ruled with him. After their death Tutankhamun and his successors restored the old gods. The names of Akhenaten and Nefertiti became hated and were removed from inscriptions, and their temples were torn down.

The mystery of the sphinx

There has been a lot of confusion about sphinxes in ancient Egypt because of Greek legends. In the Greek myth of King Oedipus, the sphinx is a ferocious and deadly female creature who destroys men who are unable to solve the riddle she gives them. But the Egyptians saw the sphinx as a lion's body with the ruler's head. The lion was a creature of the sun god and so emphasized the king's role as son of Re (p.24). The lion's strength also suggests the monarch's great power. Sometimes sphinxes combine other elements, such as the head and wings of a hawk, symbolizing the god Horus (p. 27).

SPHINX AT GIZA
This sphinx was carved about 4,500 years ago for the pharaoh Khafre and guarded the way to his pyramid.

SPHINX AND PRISONER
The way that the sphinx represents the pharaoh's power is shown in this ivory statuette, carved over 3,600 years ago.

Cobra goddess

Head cloth

Ceremonial beard

RAMSES THE GREAT
In the 13th century B.C., Ramses II reigned over Egypt for 67 years. He built more monuments and set up more statues than any other pharaoh. Among his buildings are the mortuary complex on the West Bank at Thebes, today called the Ramesseum, from which this statue comes. The king wears a royal head cloth called the nemes, above which is a crown of cobras.

Jar of sacred liquid

TUTANKHAMUN
This ruler came to the throne when only nine years old. He was obviously guided by his high officials, but seems to have been determined to bring back the old gods who had been banished by Akhenaten (see left). This famous golden mask comes from his tomb (p. 23).

TUTHMOSIS IV
This king was famous because he freed the great sphinx at Giza from the desert sand that had blown around it. He is portrayed on his knees holding two jars of sacred liquid. He is protected by the cobra goddess Wadjet on his forehead. Only kings and queens were entitled to wear cobra goddesses, who it was thought would deal out instant death by spitting flames at any enemy.

The royal court

AT GREAT STATE OCCASIONS like royal jubilee celebrations or the giving of gifts to favored courtiers, the king and court gathered together, and top officials, diplomats, and high priests would attend. Some of the courtiers were relatives of the king; some won high office through their ability as scribes. When people approached the king, they often kissed the ground at his feet. We know this because one courtier boasted that the pharaoh insisted that he kiss the royal leg and not the ground. Sometimes the pharaoh simply wanted to relax at court. King Sneferu was all set to watch 20 beautiful women from his harem row on the royal lake. It went well until one woman dropped her hair clasp in the lake, began to sulk, and stopped rowing; she refused even the king's request to carry on. The court magician had to part the waters and get the clasp from the bottom.

ROYAL HEAD
This portrait in glass was probably used as an inlay in a piece of palace furniture or as a decoration around a window.

FISHES
Children sometimes wore fishshaped amulets in their hair, possibly to guard against accidents in the Nile.

AMULET CASE
Amulets, and protective spells written on papyrus, were put in containers like this one and hung from a necklace.

OYSTER-SHELL PENDANT
The earliest jewelry in Egypt was often made of shells. Later jewelers imitated these shapes in gold. This one is carved with the name of King Senwosret.

Lion's-paw legs

ROYAL THRONE
Queen Hetepheres was the mother of King Khufu (p. 20). Her original burial place was robbed but some of her splendid furniture was reburied near her son's pyramid. The court throne was made of wood overlaid with gold leaf. Insects ate the wood away but archaeologists were able to reconstruct the furniture.

CEREMONIAL THROW STICK
Courtiers used wooden throw sticks to catch birds. This one, made of brittle faience (pottery; see p. 47), had no practical use and it was carried during ceremonies. It bears the name of Akhenaten, the pharaoh who lived in the 14th century B.C.

ROYAL VASES
The pharaohs used the best-quality utensils and cosmetic containers, which were buried in their tombs for use in the next world. These two smoothly carved mottled stone vases have lids of gold adorned with imitation twine, also in gold. They were made for King Khasekhemwy.

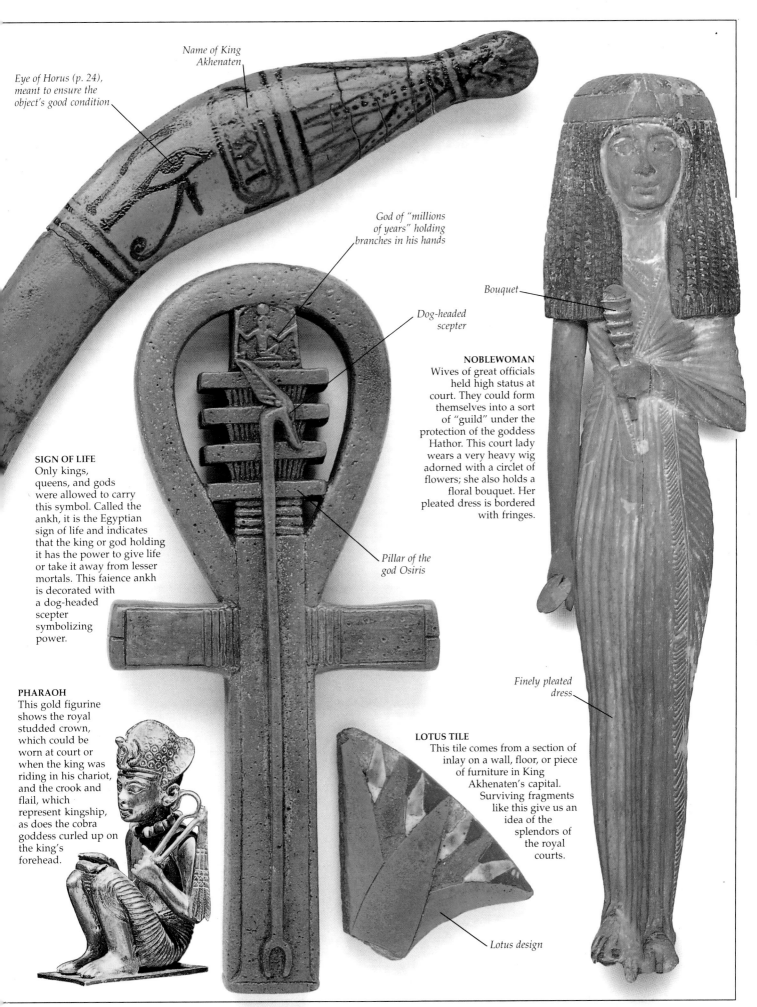

Eye of Horus (p. 24), meant to ensure the object's good condition

Name of King Akhenaten

God of "millions of years" holding branches in his hands

Dog-headed scepter

Bouquet

NOBLEWOMAN
Wives of great officials held high status at court. They could form themselves into a sort of "guild" under the protection of the goddess Hathor. This court lady wears a very heavy wig adorned with a circlet of flowers; she also holds a floral bouquet. Her pleated dress is bordered with fringes.

SIGN OF LIFE
Only kings, queens, and gods were allowed to carry this symbol. Called the ankh, it is the Egyptian sign of life and indicates that the king or god holding it has the power to give life or take it away from lesser mortals. This faience ankh is decorated with a dog-headed scepter symbolizing power.

Pillar of the god Osiris

Finely pleated dress

PHARAOH
This gold figurine shows the royal studded crown, which could be worn at court or when the king was riding in his chariot, and the crook and flail, which represent kingship, as does the cobra goddess curled up on the king's forehead.

LOTUS TILE
This tile comes from a section of inlay on a wall, floor, or piece of furniture in King Akhenaten's capital. Surviving fragments like this give us an idea of the splendors of the royal courts.

Lotus design

Preparing for the tomb

THE EGYPTIANS dreaded the thought that one day their world might cease to exist. From their belief in the power of magic, they developed a funerary cult which, in their eyes, ensured their survival forever. This involved preserving the body of the deceased. The embalmers took the body to the Beautiful House, where they worked. They made a cut in the left side of the body with a flint knife and removed the liver and lungs. These were dried out and stored in special vessels called canopic jars. The brain was also removed, but the heart was left in the body so that it could be weighed in the afterlife (p. 19). Then the body was covered with crystals of a substance called natron, which kept it from decaying, packed with dry material like leaves or sawdust, and wrapped in linen bandages.

ANUBIS
The god Anubis was supposed to be responsible for the ritual of embalming. His titles included "He who is in the place of embalming." Here he is putting the final touches on a mummified corpse.

This scarab was placed over the heart of a king to help him through the scrutiny of his past life which occurred in the underworld

Instrument for touching the mouth

Vase

WAX PLATE
Plates like this were used to cover cuts made in the flesh of the corpse. The protective eye of Horus (p. 24) symbolized the soundness of the body on which it was placed.

UTENSILS FOR "OPENING THE MOUTH"
"Opening the mouth," one of the most important of all funerary rites, restored a dead person's living faculties, allowing the mummy to eat, drink, and move around. Egyptians hated to die abroad because they knew that their corpse would not receive this rite and their afterlife would be in jeopardy. This model kit contains some of the instruments for the opening the mouth ceremony. There are vases and cups for holding and pouring sacred liquids, and a forked instrument for touching the mouth of the mummy.

OPENING THE MOUTH
A priest wearing the mask of Anubis holds the coffin upright. Behind the grieving wife and daughter, priests scatter purified water and touch the mouth of the mummy case with the ritual instruments. The eldest son burns incense and a spell is recited.

CANOPIC JARS

Any part of the body could be used in a spell against a person, so the inner organs removed during mummification were protected in special containers called canopic jars. The intestines, stomach, liver, and lungs were dried out, wrapped up in linen, and each placed in a separate jar.

MUMMY LABELS

Small wooden tags attached to mummies identified the body and gave protection. Anubis is shown on the tag on the left. He is black because black is the color of life in ancient Egypt (from the color of the fertile Nile mud).

WHAT'S INSIDE?

An X-ray of a mummy reveals the stuffing that replaced some of the organs.

NATRON

Natron, a compound of sodium carbonate and sodium bicarbonate, was used to dry out the corpse. The crystals were packed around the body, and within 40 days the corpse would be dried out and no further decay would take place. It would then be ready for wrapping in linen bandages.

Ancient linen wrapping

WITHIN THE WRAPPINGS

Unwrapping a mummy shows how the natron stopped the process of decay. This body is perfectly preserved – right down to the fingernails and toenails.

Everlasting bodies

THE FINAL STAGE in the embalming process was to put the body into its coffin. For a rich person, this could be an elaborate container made of several different, richly decorated layers. The body would then be well preserved and, as far as the Egyptians were concerned, would last forever. They thought that after a person's physical death a number of elements lived on. The most important was a person's Ka, which they thought of as the body's double and which could bring the corpse back to life. Another spirit that survived was a person's Ba, which had the head of the deceased and the body of a hawk. The Egyptians also thought that a person's shadow as well as his name had an eternal existence. The process of mummification was intended to make an everlasting body out of a corpse and to provide the Ka with a home in the afterlife. The superbly preserved bodies that have been found in Egyptian tombs show how successful the embalmers were.

HORROR HERO
The body of Ramses III, who ruled Egypt in the 12th century B.C., shows his eyes packed with linen and his arms still positioned as if holding the crook and flail scepters (p. 13). Actor Boris Karloff had his mummy costume and features modeled on Ramses III for his role in the film *The Mummy*.

Hand and arm from an Egyptian mummy, showing details of skin and nails

MUMMY CASE
Wrapped in linen bandages, the body was kept from decaying, and the family was not able to see any mistakes the embalmers might have made - for example, once a head snapped off while being fixed onto the neck with a stick, and once a queen's face was so well stuffed with pads of linen that it broke away from the rest of her head. The interior of the coffin could be richly decorated with images of gods of the underworld, while the outside could be ablaze with colorful hieroglyphs of spells destined to help the dead person in the kingdom of Osiris.

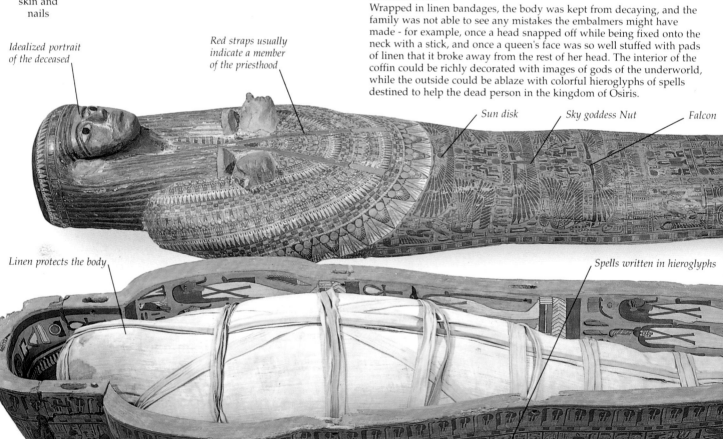

Idealized portrait of the deceased

Red straps usually indicate a member of the priesthood

Sun disk

Sky goddess Nut

Falcon

Linen protects the body

Spells written in hieroglyphs

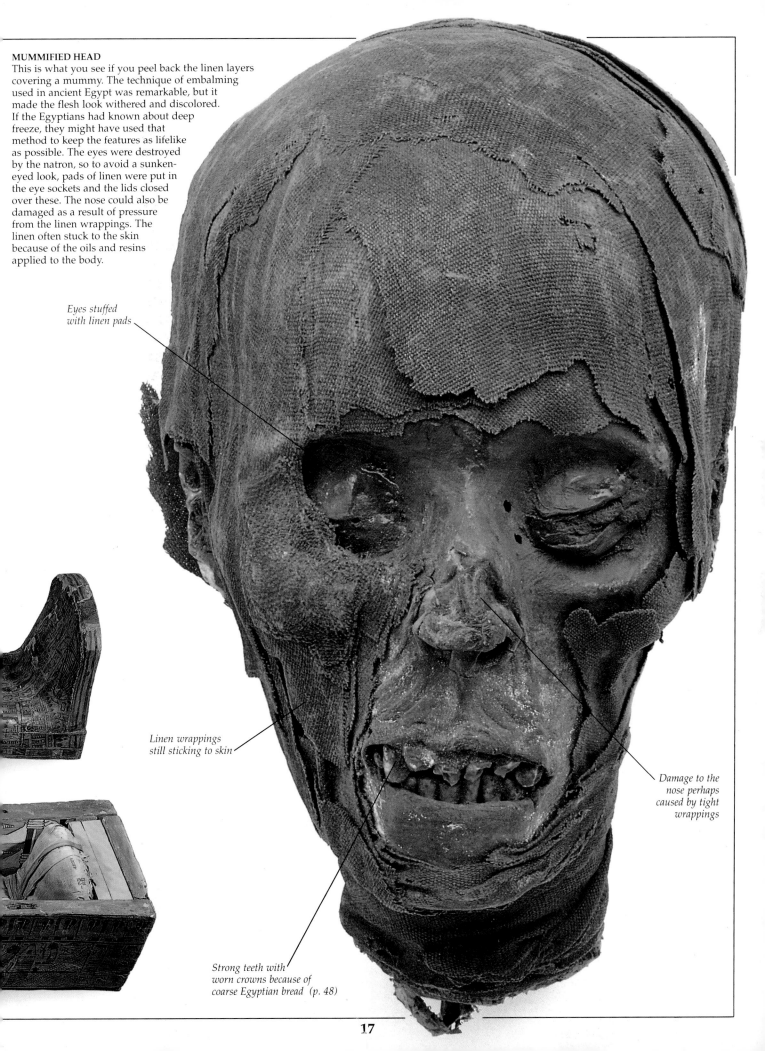

MUMMIFIED HEAD

This is what you see if you peel back the linen layers covering a mummy. The technique of embalming used in ancient Egypt was remarkable, but it made the flesh look withered and discolored. If the Egyptians had known about deep freeze, they might have used that method to keep the features as lifelike as possible. The eyes were destroyed by the natron, so to avoid a sunken-eyed look, pads of linen were put in the eye sockets and the lids closed over these. The nose could also be damaged as a result of pressure from the linen wrappings. The linen often stuck to the skin because of the oils and resins applied to the body.

Eyes stuffed with linen pads

Linen wrappings still sticking to skin

Damage to the nose perhaps caused by tight wrappings

Strong teeth with worn crowns because of coarse Egyptian bread (p. 48)

17

Journey to the afterlife

Outspread arms show that the god's power extended beyond its own body

THE ANCIENT EGYPTIANS imagined there existed an underworld below the earth, which they called Duat. Parts of it were full of perils, like poisonous snakes, lakes of fire, and executioners. Spells to counteract these dangers were often written on coffins, together with a map of the underworld. Eventually the spells and map were put on ornate scrolls of papyrus instead, which are now known as the Books of the Dead, since many were discovered on or near mummies. The book was a passport through all the dangers lurking in Duat. If you could recite the correct spells, you could pass through unharmed. The ultimate danger was to fail the test set for you in the Hall of the Two Truths, where your heart was weighed against your past deeds. The papyrus helped you as much as possible to pass the examination and reach a land that was just like Egypt itself.

HIRED MOURNERS
The more mourners at a funeral, the higher was the status of the deceased. Sometimes the family hired women to mourn at funerals. They would wave their arms, throw dust over their hair, and weep.

Ram-headed god statue covered in black resin

RAM-HEADED GOD
Sometimes statues of underworld gods were placed in the tombs in the Valley of the Kings (p. 22). With their power to ward off evil, they were meant to protect the king as he traveled through the underworld. These gods had heads of creatures such as tortoises, hippos, and rams. They are very different from other animal-headed deities (p. 24), who flourished above ground.

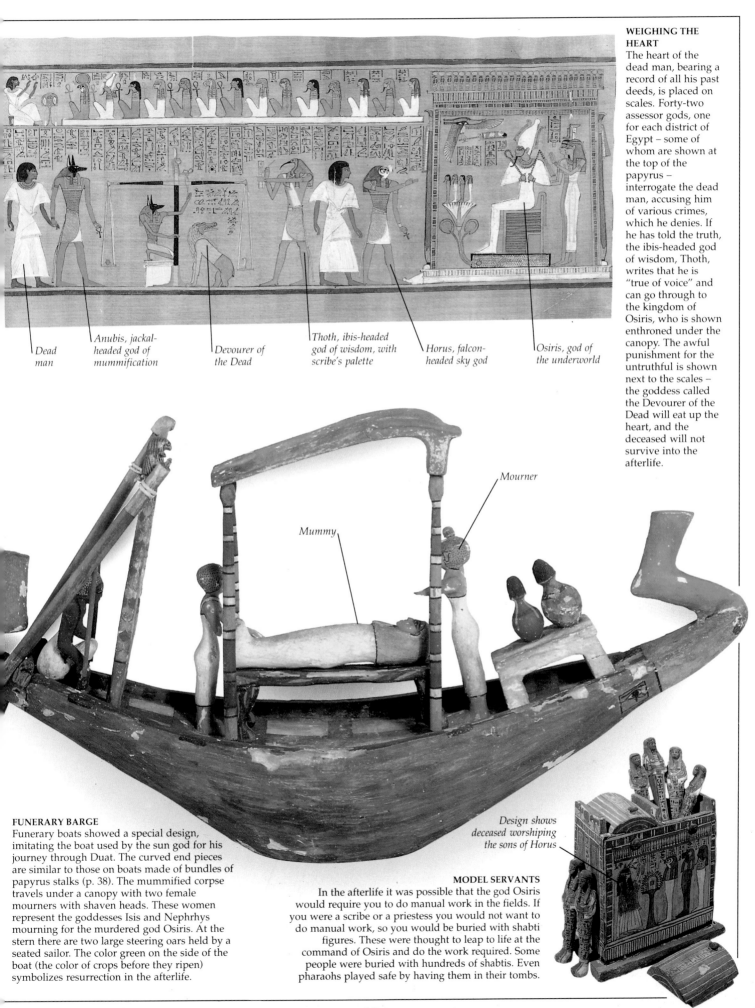

Dead man

Anubis, jackal-headed god of mummification

Devourer of the Dead

Thoth, ibis-headed god of wisdom, with scribe's palette

Horus, falcon-headed sky god

Osiris, god of the underworld

WEIGHING THE HEART

The heart of the dead man, bearing a record of all his past deeds, is placed on scales. Forty-two assessor gods, one for each district of Egypt – some of whom are shown at the top of the papyrus – interrogate the dead man, accusing him of various crimes, which he denies. If he has told the truth, the ibis-headed god of wisdom, Thoth, writes that he is "true of voice" and can go through to the kingdom of Osiris, who is shown enthroned under the canopy. The awful punishment for the untruthful is shown next to the scales – the goddess called the Devourer of the Dead will eat up the heart, and the deceased will not survive into the afterlife.

Mourner

Mummy

FUNERARY BARGE

Funerary boats showed a special design, imitating the boat used by the sun god for his journey through Duat. The curved end pieces are similar to those on boats made of bundles of papyrus stalks (p. 38). The mummified corpse travels under a canopy with two female mourners with shaven heads. These women represent the goddesses Isis and Nephrhys mourning for the murdered god Osiris. At the stern there are two large steering oars held by a seated sailor. The color green on the side of the boat (the color of crops before they ripen) symbolizes resurrection in the afterlife.

Design shows deceased worshiping the sons of Horus

MODEL SERVANTS

In the afterlife it was possible that the god Osiris would require you to do manual work in the fields. If you were a scribe or a priestess you would not want to do manual work, so you would be buried with shabti figures. These were thought to leap to life at the command of Osiris and do the work required. Some people were buried with hundreds of shabtis. Even pharaohs played safe by having them in their tombs.

The great pyramids

THE FIRST PYRAMID was built as the burial place of King Djoser c. 2630 B.C., by his gifted architect Imhotep (pp. 34-35). It rose in six stages, and is called the Step Pyramid. It was supposed to represent a gigantic stairway for the king to climb to join the sun god in the sky. Some later kings had step pyramids too, but during the reign of King Sneferu the true pyramid, with sloping sides, developed. The idea of this pyramid was to re-create the mound that had emerged out of the watery ground at the beginning of time, on which the sun god stood and brought the other gods and goddesses into being. The largest pyramid of all is the Great Pyramid at Giza, built for King Khufu c. 2528 B.C. The pyramids were intended to protect the bodies of the pharaohs buried deep inside them. Later pyramids contained inscriptions of spells to help the pharaoh in the afterlife. Doors of granite and false passages were constructed to deter robbers who came in pursuit of the rich offerings buried with the kings. But by c. 1000 B.C. all the pyramids had been robbed of their precious contents.

CLIMBERS
Today there is a law in Egypt forbidding visitors from climbing the Great Pyramid. But in the 19th century many people felt the urge to climb the pyramid and admire the view below. It was not difficult to climb, but if you slipped, it was almost impossible to regain your footing.

GRAND GALLERY
This gallery, 154 ft (47 m) long and 28 ft (8.5 m) high, rises toward the burial chamber. It has an elaborate stone roof. After the burial, great blocks of granite were slid down the gallery to seal off the burial chamber. The pharaoh's sarcophagus could not have been pulled up the gallery into the burial chamber – it is wider than the gallery and must have been constructed when the pyramid was being built.

Small pyramids, the burial places of the three chief wives of Khufu

Mortuary temple, where offerings could be made

THE GREAT PYRAMID
Built for King Khufu about 4,500 years ago, the Great Pyramid was one of the seven Wonders of the Ancient World. It contains over 2.3 million limestone blocks ranging from 2.5 to 15 tons. The builders may have had levers to help get the stones into place, but they had no pulleys or other machinery. The whole pyramid probably took about 20 years to build. There was a standing work force of craftsmen and laborers, which swelled every year for three months when the Nile flooded and the field workers were sent on national service to help with the construction work. The pyramids were just one part of the funerary complex devoted to the pharaoh's afterlife. There was also a mortuary temple for cult offerings and a causeway leading to the valley temple – the place where the king's body was received after its last journey along the Nile River.

Causeway connecting pyramid to temple in Nile valley

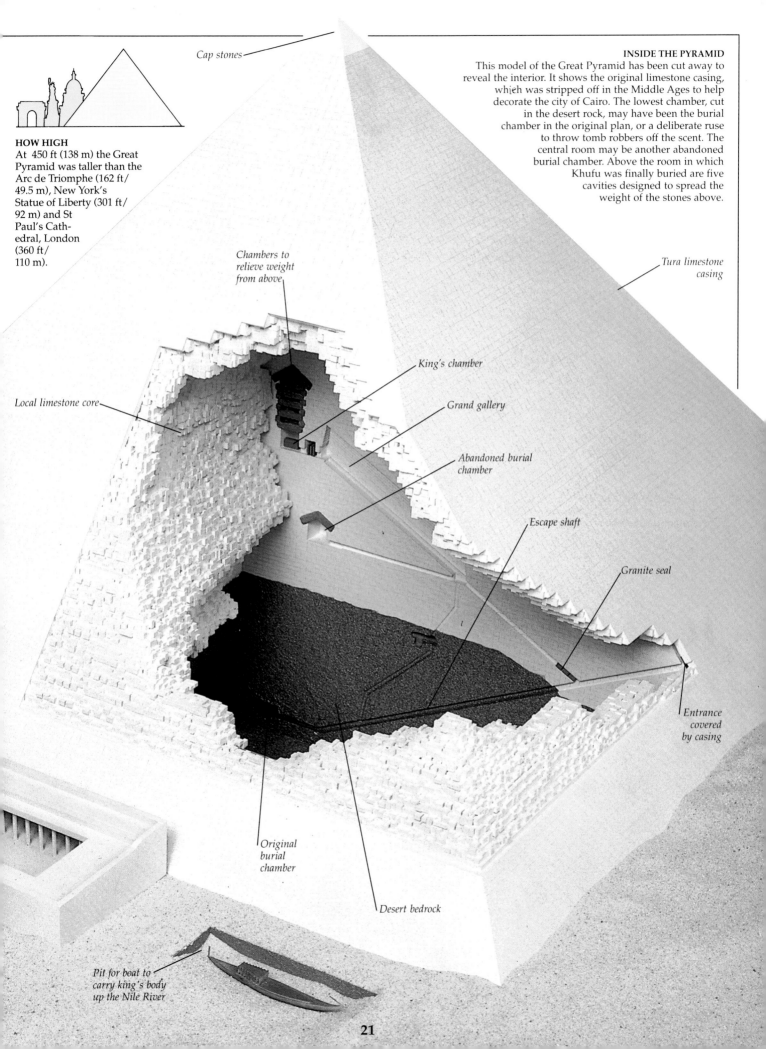

Cap stones

HOW HIGH
At 450 ft (138 m) the Great Pyramid was taller than the Arc de Triomphe (162 ft/ 49.5 m), New York's Statue of Liberty (301 ft/ 92 m) and St Paul's Cathedral, London (360 ft/ 110 m).

INSIDE THE PYRAMID
This model of the Great Pyramid has been cut away to reveal the interior. It shows the original limestone casing, which was stripped off in the Middle Ages to help decorate the city of Cairo. The lowest chamber, cut in the desert rock, may have been the burial chamber in the original plan, or a deliberate ruse to throw tomb robbers off the scent. The central room may be another abandoned burial chamber. Above the room in which Khufu was finally buried are five cavities designed to spread the weight of the stones above.

Tura limestone casing

Chambers to relieve weight from above

King's chamber

Grand gallery

Abandoned burial chamber

Local limestone core

Escape shaft

Granite seal

Original burial chamber

Desert bedrock

Entrance covered by casing

Pit for boat to carry king's body up the Nile River

The Valley of the Kings

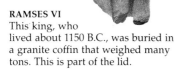

RAMSES VI
This king, who lived about 1150 B.C., was buried in a granite coffin that weighed many tons. This is part of the lid.

THE PYRAMID AGE drew to a close around 2150 B.C. Nearly all the pharaohs from Tuthmosis I (1504 B.C.) to Ramses XI (1070 B.C.) chose to be buried in tombs in the Valley of the Kings. Far away from the flood plain, the valley lay deep in the cliffs to the west of the Nile. There was a ridge in front of the entrance where guards were posted. Some of the tombs were placed high in the cliffside in an attempt to conceal their entrances from robbers; others had elaborate doors and were much more obvious. The usual pattern was for the tomb to have a deep corridor – known as the Way of the Sun God – with a well or shaft near the inner end that was intended to catch rainwater and to deter tomb robbers. Beyond this was the Hall of Gold, where the king was buried. He was surrounded by gilded furniture and jewelry, royal clothing, and regalia (crook, scepter, etc.). The contents of the tomb of Tutankhamun were the only ones to escape the hands of robbers before c. 1000 B.C.

UNDERWORLD DEITY
This hippopotamus-headed god was found in the tomb of Tuthmosis III. It is covered in a black resin. It looks ferocious, but its anger is directed only at the king's enemies. It probably represented one of the guardians of the secret doors of the mansion of the god Osiris.

SACRED SERPENT
The valley was thought to be protected by a goddess, called Meretseger, who was portrayed as a cobra. The tomb workers thought she would blind or poison criminals and those who swore false oaths.

VALLEY VIEW
This view of the Valley of the Kings by the 19th-century artist David Roberts conveys something of the solitude of the place. Today it is much busier, with a modern road, parking lot, and the stalls of souvenir sellers destroying the ancient atmosphere.

FOREMAN AND HIS SON
Foremen like Anherkhau, shown here with his son, were responsible for making sure that the metal tools were distributed to the workers. They also had to organize the crew in the tomb so that the stonecutters would be immediately followed by the plasterers and painters, and the flow of work would not stop. This picture of Anherkhau comes from his own colorfully painted tomb.

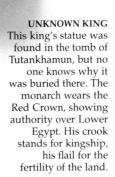

DEIR EL MEDINA
These stone foundations are all that is left of Deir el Medina, the village where the tomb workers lived. Founded in the 16th century B.C., the village flourished for 500 years – as long as the kings continued to be buried in the valley. Usually about 60 families lived in these houses.

UNKNOWN KING
This king's statue was found in the tomb of Tutankhamun, but no one knows why it was buried there. The monarch wears the Red Crown, showing authority over Lower Egypt. His crook stands for kingship, his flail for the fertility of the land.

Tutankhamun's tomb

The resting place of the young king Tutankhamun was the only tomb of a New Kingdom pharaoh (the New Kingdom lasted 1570-1090 B.C.) to escape almost untouched by robbers. It was found by Howard Carter in 1922, the last of the valley tombs to be discovered. Its contents included weapons, clothes, furniture, jewelry, musical instruments, and model boats, as well as the king's famous coffins and mask (p. 11). Many of these items were made of solid gold or were richly decorated with gold leaf. The king was buried with his two stillborn daughters and a lock of hair of his grandmother Queen Tiye.

ALL DRESSED UP
The delicate items discovered in Tutankhamun's tomb had to be carefully prepared for transport to the Cairo Museum. Archaeologists Howard Carter and Lord Carnarvon are here wrapping up one of the guardian statues from the tomb.

Gods and goddesses

THE EGYPTIANS worshiped hundreds of different gods and goddesses, and sometimes it is difficult to work out who was who. Many of the gods are represented by animals. For example, a baboon might stand for Thoth, god of wisdom, at one temple, and a moon god called Khonsu at another. Each of the 42 different administrative districts, or nomes, had its own god, and there were many others besides. Overall, the sun god was the dominant deity in Egyptian religion, although he could take different forms. At dawn he would be Khepri, the scarab beetle rolling the sun disk above the eastern horizon. He could then become Re-Harakhty, the great hawk soaring in the sky. He was seen as responsible for all creation – people, animals, the fertility of the soil, and the king's journey through the underworld. As Amun-Re he was king of the gods and protector of the pharaoh when he went on military campaigns. The pharaoh Akhenaten saw the sun god as a disk with rays ending in human hands holding the sign of life (p. 13). During his reign all other gods were banished, but his son-in-law Tutankhamun restored them (pp.10-11).

THE GODS AND THEIR MAKERS
This detail from a 19th-century painting shows the artist's idea of a workshop in which Egyptian figures of the gods were made. The cat is modeling for an image of Bastet (opposite).

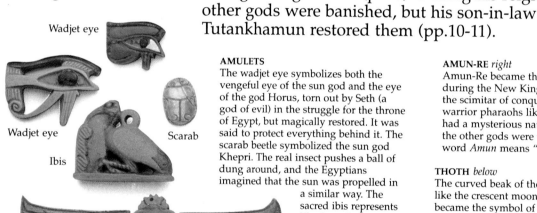

Wadjet eye

Wadjet eye

Ibis

Scarab

Winged scarab

AMULETS
The wadjet eye symbolizes both the vengeful eye of the sun god and the eye of the god Horus, torn out by Seth (a god of evil) in the struggle for the throne of Egypt, but magically restored. It was said to protect everything behind it. The scarab beetle symbolized the sun god Khepri. The real insect pushes a ball of dung around, and the Egyptians imagined that the sun was propelled in a similar way. The sacred ibis represents Thoth, god of wisdom and healing.

AMUN-RE *right*
Amun-Re became the principal god during the New Kingdom. He handed the scimitar of conquest to great warrior pharaohs like Tuthmosis III. He had a mysterious nature, which even the other gods were unaware of – the word *Amun* means "hidden."

THOTH *below*
The curved beak of the ibis was like the crescent moon, so the bird became the symbol of the moon god Thoth. He was the patron of the scribes, and gave the Egyptians knowledge of writing, medicine, and mathematics.

ANUBIS
Jackals used to haunt cemeteries, so they were linked with funerals - the idea being that a jackal god would protect the domain of the dead. Anubis also supervised embalming (p. 14) and looked after the place where mummification was done.

GODS OF PROSPERITY
These figures are tying together lotus and papyrus – the plants of Upper and Lower Egypt – around the hieroglyph meaning "unite." Often called the Nile gods, these figures were symbols of the fertility that came from the river's annual flood.

FACE TO FACE
The king of Egypt was the embodiment of the god Horus and was therefore thought to be divine himself. This relief shows Tuthmosis III before the god. The hawk-headed god was also a solar deity - the hawk high in the sky whose eyes were thought of as the sun and moon. The name Horus in Egyptian meant "he who is far above."

BASTET
The cat goddess Bastet was the daughter of Re, the sun god. She represented the power of the sun to ripen crops. Many bronze cat figures were dedicated in her now ruined temple in the northeast Delta.

OSIRIS
Osiris, called "foremost of the westerners," because most of the cemeteries were situated in the west, was god of the underworld. His kingdom, beyond the perilous regions below the earth, was thought to look like Egypt.

Silver necklace with wadjet eye

Scarab

Crook and flail scepters, showing that Osiris is king of the underworld

Crown of reeds and ostrich feathers

KHNUM
The ram-headed god Khnum presided over the hazardous Nile cataracts (rapids). It was on his word that the god Hapy rose to cause the yearly flood of the river.

25

Magic and medicine

THE GODS OF THE TEMPLES played little part in the lives of ordinary Egyptians, so many people used magic to ease problems like the dangers of childbirth, infant mortality, and fevers. The Egyptians also had great medical skill. Physicians' papyrus manuals survive which describe how to treat ailments and reveal a detailed knowledge of anatomy. They wrote about the importance of the heart and how it "speaks out" through the back of the head and hands – a reference to the pulse beat. There were remedies for eye disorders, tumors, and some physical complaints. The Egyptians believed that many diseases came from wormlike creatures invading the body. Physicians and magicians worked together, using both medicines and spells for problems like snake bites and scorpion stings. They also used magic to ward off possible injuries from crocodiles or the ghosts of the dead. Letters to the dead could be written on pottery bowls and put in tombs if a person felt that a dead relative's spirit was upset or likely to cause trouble. Dangers were also counteracted by amulets, or magical charms.

Panel from the tomb of Hesire, the king's dentist in c. 2700 B.C.

Headrest amulet

AMULETS
Magical charms could be worn on necklaces and bracelets while a person was alive, and placed on the person's corpse in the mummy wrappings to give protection in the next life. They were supposed to ward off injury and were some-times accompanied by spells.

Pillar amulet

Knot amulet

Powerful plants

Plants played an integral part in both magic and medicine. Juniper berries were valued enough to be imported from Lebanon. Garlic was prized for its medicinal properties and was used in magic, too.

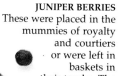

LOTUS
The lotus was very important to the Egyptians – they decorated their temples and many of their belongings with images of the lotus.

Lotus blossom

JUNIPER BERRIES
These were placed in the mummies of royalty and courtiers or were left in baskets in their tombs. The juice was used in the purification rituals performed over the corpse.

HEAR OUR PRAYER
On this stela (stone tablet) is a prayer to the god Ptah, and ears to help him hear it.

GODDESS OF CHILDBIRTH
Prayers to the goddess Taweret were an essential part of giving birth. She was shown as a pregnant hippopotamus and sometimes looked ferocious – this was to keep evil from attacking the woman as she gave birth. Magic liquid could be poured from her breast.

HENNA
Henna, used to color the hair and skin, was supposed to have the power to ward off danger.

GARLIC
Garlic was used in burials. It was also thought to repel snakes and expel tapeworms.

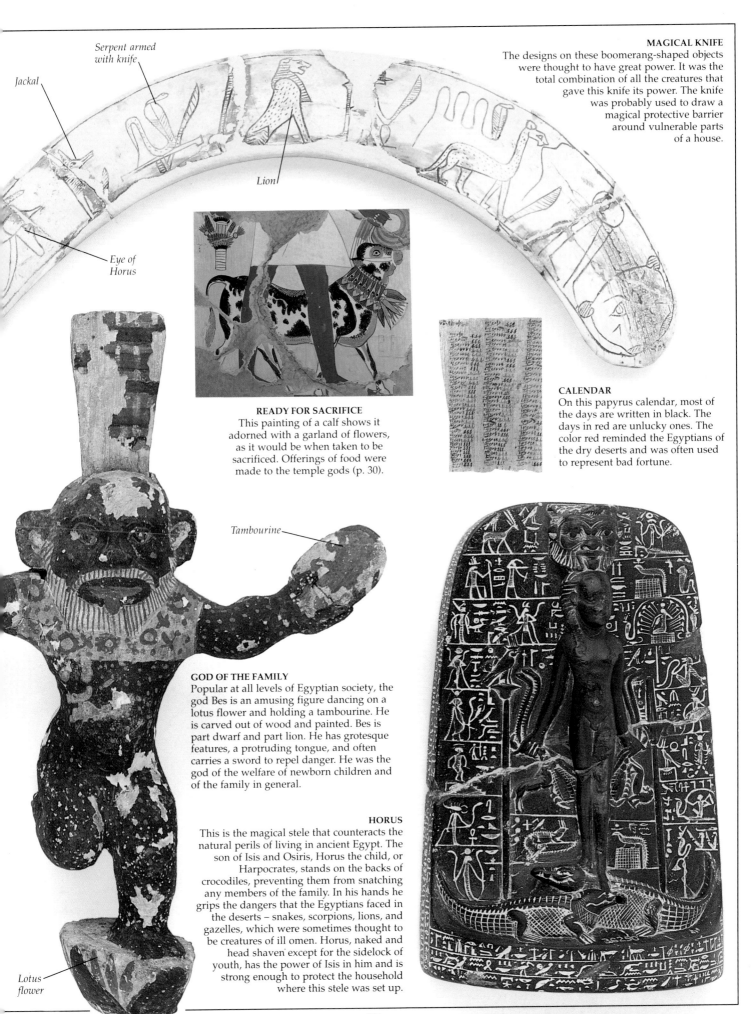

Serpent armed with knife

Jackal

Eye of Horus

Lion

MAGICAL KNIFE
The designs on these boomerang-shaped objects were thought to have great power. It was the total combination of all the creatures that gave this knife its power. The knife was probably used to draw a magical protective barrier around vulnerable parts of a house.

READY FOR SACRIFICE
This painting of a calf shows it adorned with a garland of flowers, as it would be when taken to be sacrificed. Offerings of food were made to the temple gods (p. 30).

CALENDAR
On this papyrus calendar, most of the days are written in black. The days in red are unlucky ones. The color red reminded the Egyptians of the dry deserts and was often used to represent bad fortune.

Tambourine

GOD OF THE FAMILY
Popular at all levels of Egyptian society, the god Bes is an amusing figure dancing on a lotus flower and holding a tambourine. He is carved out of wood and painted. Bes is part dwarf and part lion. He has grotesque features, a protruding tongue, and often carries a sword to repel danger. He was the god of the welfare of newborn children and of the family in general.

HORUS
This is the magical stele that counteracts the natural perils of living in ancient Egypt. The son of Isis and Osiris, Horus the child, or Harpocrates, stands on the backs of crocodiles, preventing them from snatching any members of the family. In his hands he grips the dangers that the Egyptians faced in the deserts – snakes, scorpions, lions, and gazelles, which were sometimes thought to be creatures of ill omen. Horus, naked and head shaven except for the sidelock of youth, has the power of Isis in him and is strong enough to protect the household where this stele was set up.

Lotus flower

27

Priests and temples

IN THEORY, the pharaoh was supposed to act as the high priest in every temple in Egypt, but since that was impractical, his duties were usually carried out by the chief priest. In the great temples such as Karnak at Thebes, sacred to Amun-Re, king of the gods, the chief priest had great power and controlled the vast wealth in the temple treasuries and the great lands of the temple estates. It was possible for the office of chief priest to remain in the hands of one family for generations until the pharaoh broke their hold by making an appointment from outside. The priests had titles to indicate their power – they were called God's Servant, with the addition of First, Second, or Third, to show their position. Priests at lower levels were called Pure Ones or God's Fathers, and had the responsibility of serving on the temple rota system, maintaining the temple's property, and keeping administrative records.

FEED THE BIRDS
Ibises, sacred to the god Thoth, were revered in Egypt. This detail from a fanciful 19th-century painting shows ibises being fed by a priestess.

Sidelock of hair

KNEELING PRIEST
This type of priest was called a Yun-mutef priest, meaning "Pillar of his Mother." He symbolizes the divine child Horus (p. 27), wears a leopard skin, and has his hair in a sidelock to represent youth. He kneels at an offering table.

Offering table

Paw and tail of leopard skin

FALSE DOOR
Courtiers had tomb chapels with false doors, which stood for the idea of contact between the tomb and the place where offerings to the gods could be made. "Soul priests" would leave offerings of food and drink at these doors - on this door several bearers are shown bringing meat, poultry, and bread to the tomb.

THE TEMPLE OF DENDERA
The goddess Hathor's temple as it survives today was built during the time when Egypt was ruled by the Greeks and Romans (pp. 62-63) – in fact, Queen Cleopatra is shown on its rear wall. The heads belong to the goddess Hathor.

LAST OF THE TEMPLES
This detail of a painting by David Roberts, who traveled widely in Egypt in the 19th century, shows the temple of Isis on the island of Philae. This was the last Egyptian temple to fall to the Christians. The Roman emperor Justinian closed it in the 6th century A.D., and ordered it to be turned into a church.

COLOSSAL CARVINGS
Near the second cataract (rapids) of the Nile at Abu Simbel in Nubia, Ramses II ordered two temples to be carved out of the sandstone cliffs. This one was carved for himself and three major Egyptian gods – Amun, Re-Harakhty, and Ptah. Huge statues of Ramses flank the entrance.

Obelisks

The Egyptians carved stone obelisks with the titles of their kings and dedications to the gods. The pointed tip of the obelisk represents the ground on which the sun god stood to create the universe.

GATEPOST
This obelisk was one of two that stood at the entrance to the temple at Luxor. The other obelisk was given to the king of France and is now in the Place de la Concorde, Paris.

THINKER
This priest seems to have a worried expression. In fact, the lines on his forehead, bags under his eyes, and furrows around his mouth are meant to indicate a life of serious contemplation. He is bald because most priests had to remove their hair.

Winged sky goddess

Son of Horus who looked after mummified body of priestess

GOLDEN COFFIN
This is the coffin of a priestess who served the god Amun and performed songs in his honor during temple rituals. She had three coffins, of which this one, of gilded wood, is the most impressive. Her face is portrayed as she would have wanted to look for eternity.

Sacred rituals

A SELECT FEW PRIESTS were involved in the ceremonies that took place in the temple's sanctuary. Accompanied by burning incense and lamps, and scattering purified water from the temple's sacred lake, the high priest approached the shrine, saying "I am a pure one." He would break the clay seal on the door of the shrine, and open it to reveal the gold statue of the god. This he would decorate before making an offering of food. The priests then left the sanctuary with someone sweeping the floor as they went out, so as not to leave any trace of their presence.

SACRED BUCKET
This bronze container, called a situla, held holy water from the sacred lake of the temple. It was used in ceremonies involving the sprinkling of holy water. It is decorated with images of various gods and ancestral rulers of Egypt.

Crescent and full moons worshiped by baboons

VERDIGRIS VASE
Metal vases were used to pour sacred water over offering tables, to show the purity of the offerings made to the god or goddess. They also held a mixture of water and natron (p. 15), used for ritual washing before and after eating at a temple festival or ritual.

WORSHIPER
This priestess, a woman called Deniu-en-Khons, is making offerings to the god Re-Harakhty. The falcon-headed god is carrying the ankh, the Egyptian sign of life, as well as the royal symbols of crook and flail.

Tapered base allowing situla to rest on a stand

Cup in which incense was burned

Container for pellets of incense

PRIESTLY PROCESSION
This group of priests is bald – priests shaved off their hair to ensure cleanliness. Their leader is carrying an incense burner and scattering sacred water.

Baboon

Bird

Jackal

Frog

MAKING OFFERINGS
This bronze plaque shows a priest pouring sacred water over some offerings. Round loaves of bread and a vase of liquid are being offered to the god. At the front is a channel through which the holy water could drain away.

One of many temple paintings showing incense burners in use

AIR FRESHENER
Incense burns with an aroma that rises with the smoke. It was used in temples to attract the attention of the god with a pleasant fragrance, and to purify the atmosphere in the temple. This bronze incense burner has the head of the hawk god at one end.

STANDARD ORNAMENT
Priests carried standards in their processions through the temples. All that has survived of these are the emblems on top of the supporting poles. This one shows a bundle of papyrus plants and is topped by the falcon god Horus, who is identified with the king of Egypt. Horus wears the combined crowns of Upper and Lower Egypt.

Goddess Mut

Head of Hathor

Khonsu

CULT MIRROR
Objects normally used for beautification, such as mirrors and cosmetic palettes, were placed in the temples for the use of the god. This example has a design that is full of religious symbols. From its handle, a crescent rises toward a hawk, suggesting a moon god such as Khonsu. Heads of the goddess Hathor adorn the columns on the face of the mirror itself. The goddess Mut (wife of the king of the gods and mother of Khonsu) is the figure being presented with a mirror in the center.

Ivory handle

31

Scribes and scholars

SCRIBES WERE NEAR THE TOP of Egyptian society, and capable scribes could do very well – one, Horemheb, even became king. Students were trained rigorously for about five years, beginning at the age of nine. This was often a problem because the young pupils could see children of their own age playing in the fields. Papyri have been discovered containing reprimands from senior to junior scribes about neglecting lessons; sometimes physical punishment was recommended. One form of encouragement offered to pupils was a list of the drawbacks of other professions – exaggerated, of course. For example, jewelers and metalworkers were said to choke in the heat of their furnaces; weavers had to put up with cramped conditions. But the scribe could look forward to authority, freedom from taxes and national service during times of flood, and immortality through his writings.

Hole for ink

READY FOR WORK
This young scribe is shown sitting cross-legged with his papyrus scroll on his knees. Scribes are usually shown seated like this in Egyptian art.

Bushy top of plant

GOOSE CENSUS
This scribe is counting geese on a nobleman's estate. He will enter the total on his scroll, for taxation records. His basket-work "briefcase" is in front of him, and his palettes and brushes are under his arm.

PAPYRUS
This triangular-stemmed reed, which grew about 13 ft (4 m) tall, flourished along the banks of the Nile, but vanished due to overharvesting for boats, baskets, sandals, rope, and writing material. Attempts are now being made to reintroduce it into Egypt.

Stem used for writing material

Outer rind peeled away

Alternate layers

Inner pith cut into strips

Stone

Mallet

MAKING A PAPYRUS SHEET
The strips of pith were arranged in two layers, one set horizontal, the next vertical, on top of each other. They were covered with linen, and heavy pressure was applied with stones or a mallet. Eventually the strips would weld together in their own sap.

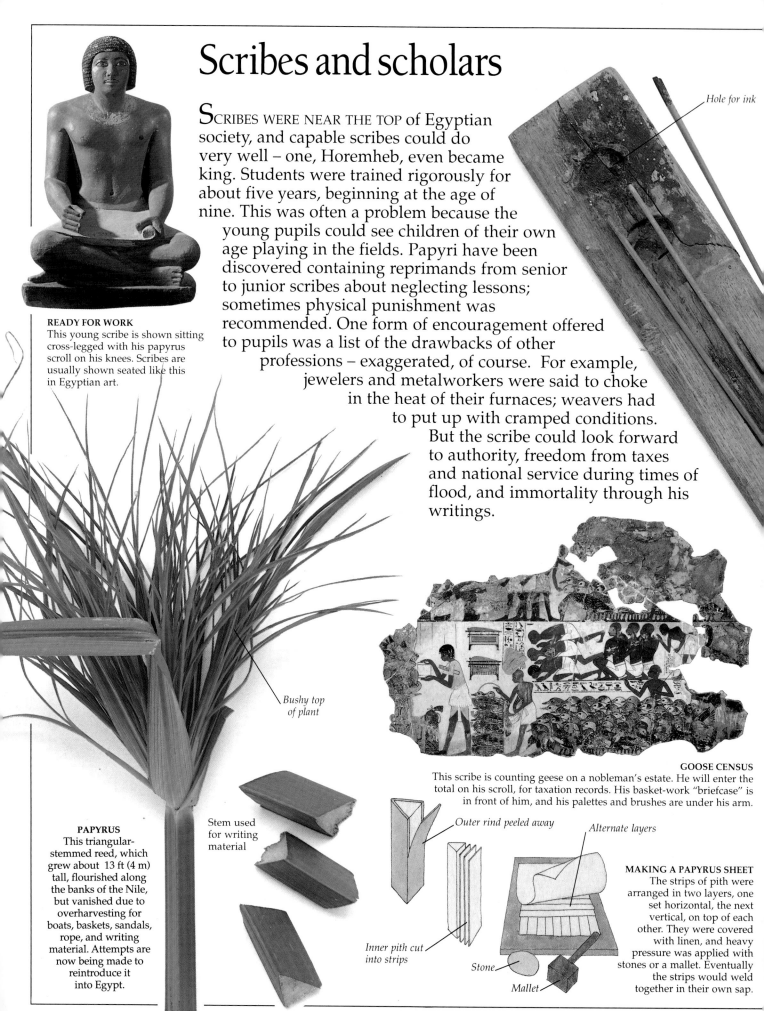

Grinder for crushing pigments

BASALT PALETTE
This palette is inscribed with a royal name, indicating that the scribe who used it was in the service of the palace. The pigments could be made from charcoal or soot to produce black, or from red ocher, or blue or green minerals.

Draughtsmen
Egyptian artists were professional scribes who specialized in draftsmanship for royal or funerary monuments. From unfinished tombs like that of King Horemheb it is possible to see all the stages involved in painting. First junior draftsmen drew the scenes in red ocher on the dry plaster. Next senior artists made corrections in black outline. The painters would then fill in the outlines with color, or sculptors would cut away the background plaster to form a relief for painting.

SKETCH PAD
A red ocher grid allowed the artist to divide the human body into squares to ensure the right proportions in this practice drawing of King Tuthmosis III.

WOODEN PALETTE
Most scribes had a wooden palette like this. It was portable, because the scribe might have to travel on business or to gather taxes.

Name of Ramses I

SCRIBES AND SUPERVISOR
Busy writing on their scrolls, these two scribes appear to be recording the words of the standing overseer. Notice the "briefcase" and document container in front of them.

Reed brushes for precision writing

SIGN FOR SCRIBE
This hieroglyphic sign shows a brush holder, a water pot for mixing pigments, and a palette, together making up the Egyptian word for a qualified scribe. The word was pronounced "sesh."

BRUSHES
The thick rope brush made of papyrus twine was used by painters covering large wall surfaces in tombs or temples. The other is also a painter's brush, perhaps used to paint thick hieroglyphs on huge statues.

Writing

S CRIBES HAD TO BE EXPERTS in writing hieroglyphs, an elaborate form of picture-writing using about 700 different signs. It was deliberately kept complicated so that not many people could master it and scribes could keep their special position. Hieroglyphs were used on state monuments, temples, tombs, and religious papyri. They could be written from left to right, right to left, or top to bottom. For business contracts, letters, and stories, scribes used a different form of writing (script), called hieratic, which was a fast-written version of hieroglyphs, always running from right to left. Later on an even more rapid script evolved, called demotic. Demotic was often used for legal documents. At the end of the Egyptian civilization, scribes also had to be able to write Greek, the language of their overlords.

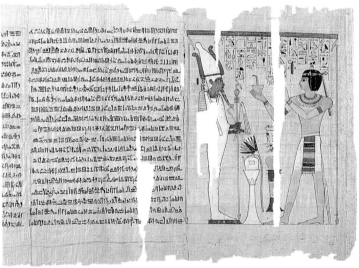

TWO SCRIPTS
On papyrus, scribes usually used the fast form of writing called hieratic. On this example, hieroglyphs appear above the picture of a high priest making an offering to the god Osiris. To the left is the script in hieratic.

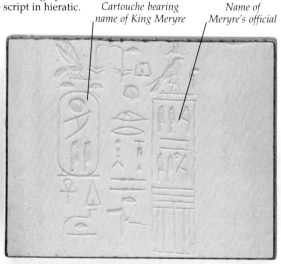

IMHOTEP
This talented scribe lived 4,500 years ago. He was High Priest of the sun god as well as the designer of the first pyramid, at Saqqara. After his death he became accredited with limitless wisdom and was eventually turned into a god. Here he is unrolling a papyrus scroll.

ROYAL DOOR PLATE
The hieroglyphs on this metal plate read: "There shall always exist the Son of Re whom he loves, Amenhotep the god, ruler of Thebes."

King's name contained in oval border called a cartouche

CYLINDER SEAL
Seals like this were an early way of proving ownership or authority. This one bears the name of King Meryre, and also the name of one of his officials, who was obviously the owner of the seal. To the right is an impression showing the complete surface of the seal.

Cartouche bearing name of King Meryre

Name of Meryre's official

Top   Underside   Small scarab

SCARABS
The beetle, symbolizing the sun god (p. 24), was often carved on the tops of stamp seals. The underside could include names, titles, or information that the owner could stamp on clay or papyrus. The large scarab tells us that Amenhotep III killed 102 lions during his reign.

The Rosetta Stone
When the last temple was closed, in the 6th century A.D., the skill of reading hieroglyphs was lost until the discovery of this stone in 1799. On the stone are three scripts. The bottom section is in Greek, the center in demotic, and the top in hieroglyphs. The stone was first set up in a temple. It was an elaborate "thank you" to the Greek ruler of Egypt, Ptolemy V, who reigned in the 2nd century B.C., for favors that he had given to the priests. The three scripts contained the same text, allowing the hieroglyphs to be translated.

HIEROGLYPHS AND THEIR ORIGINS
Scribes chose pictures of their script from the world around them. The barn owl represented the consonant "m"; on the carving in the picture it forms part of the royal name "Amen em hat."

JEAN-FRANÇOIS CHAMPOLLION
French archeologist, Jean-François Champollion spent many years deciphering the symbols on a slab of basalt found at Rosetta in the western Delta. His work on the Rosetta stone, as it is now called, was an important breakthrough in the translation of ancient hieroglyphics.

DECIPHERING THE STONE
When it was known that the stone contained royal names such as Ptolemy, their equivalents in hieroglyphs could be found at the top of the stone. From this information, the hieroglyphs for other words were worked out and the text was gradually deciphered.

NOTEBOOK
Some hieroglyphic signs required a lot of practice by pupil scribes. Here a scribe has got carried away drawing the duckling hieroglyph, which was used in writing the word for "prime minister." The scribe has also practiced drawing the head of a lion, which is used in one of the scenes in the Book of the Dead.

Weapons of war

SOLDIERS FIRST PLAYED an important role in Egypt around 3000 B.C. Later, the pharaohs undertook military campaigns abroad in Palestine, Syria, and Nubia. The Egyptian army was well organized. It had a hierarchy of officers, from the pharaoh himself down to officers in charge of groups of 50 soldiers, and army scribes who wrote dispatches and records of the campaigns. There were both infantry and chariot troops. Egyptian chariots, each manned by two soldiers and pulled by two horses, were made of wood. They acted as mobile firing platforms from which archers could attack the enemy. In peacetime, soldiers would take part in civil tasks such as digging irrigation canals or transporting stone from the desert for the king's tomb.

Ceremonial axe with openwork head

Long blade for slicing action

Battle-axe

KING AT WAR
This scene from the side of a box discovered in Tutankhamun's tomb shows the king attacking enemies from Nubia. His foes are falling in disarray. He rides in a chariot drawn by two horses, followed by fan bearers. In real life the king had a charioteer to drive for him.

Silver-shafted axe

ANCIENT AXES
The axe was used as a weapon all over the Middle East. The silver-handled axe has a long blade designed for a slicing motion. The openwork axe is ceremonial, but could also have made an effective weapon, like the plainer axe to the right.

Silver nail

FINGER GUARD
Archers would sometimes draw their bow strings into a triangular shape, pulling them back to their ears. This bone guard protected the archer's finger from pain caused by the taut string (made of animal gut) as he drew his bow.

Flint heads

SMALL BUT DEADLY
The first arrowheads were made of flint or a hard wood like ebony. Later bronze was used. The horseshoe shapes were designed to wound, and the sharp triangular arrowheads were meant to kill the victim outright.

Bronze heads

TRUSTY BLADES
Inspired by a Middle Eastern design, swords had smoother handles than daggers. They had the advantage that they could be gripped tightly; they could also have a longer blade, attached with rivets.

ON THE MARCH
Protected by large shields made of wood rather than heavy armor, these infantry soldiers are armed with battle-axes and spears.

ARROW
With its blunt tip and reed shaft, this arrow may have been a hunter's weapon, though it is the size of a soldier's arrow.

Dagger

MEDALS
Gold flies were given to a soldier who had done well in combat, persistently "stinging" the enemy.

DEADLY DAGGER
Traditional Egyptian daggers have fine, tapered copper blades decorated with stripes. The wide top of the blade is riveted to the handle. The pommel of ivory or bone on top of the handle fitted into the palm of the hand. Daggers could be carried openly in the belt of a kilt or in wooden sheaths overlaid with gold.

Tutankhamun wears a wrist protector

Short sword

Long sword

WRIST PROTECTOR
An archer wore this guard on his left wrist to protect himself from the whip of the bowstring when firing an arrow. The tongue-shaped section extended into the palm.

Sailing on the Nile

THE NILE was the main highway of Egypt. The earliest boats were made of papyrus, but dockyards along the Nile were soon busy making boats out of timber. The best example of the skill of the Egyptian shipbuilder is a boat over 130 ft (40 m) long built for King Khufu around 4,500 years ago and discovered in a pit next to the Great Pyramid (pp. 20–21). It was a keel-less ceremonial barge with a cabin for the king and was probably intended for Khufu's journey with the sun-god in the afterlife. Temple reliefs show other large boats transporting huge columns and obelisks of granite from the quarries of Aswan. The Egyptians had a full range of boats for transportation on the Nile, from small cargo boats for carrying grain to state ships for kings and high officials. The Egyptians gave ships names like we do today. For example, one commander started off in a ship called *Northern* and got promoted to the ship *Rising in Memphis*.

THE RA EXPEDITION
The first Egyptian boats were made of papyrus stalks bunched together. If they got waterlogged they could easily be replaced using the plentiful reeds. Explorer Thor Heyerdahl sailed his papyrus boat *Ra* from Egypt to America. He did not prove that the Egyptians made this journey, but he showed that it was possible.

GONE FISHING
These skiffs are made of bundles of papyrus reeds tied together with twine. They are each propelled by two oarsmen and are linked to each other by the dragnet. You can see some of the fish trapped in the net as well as the floats around the edges of it. The fishermen are about to pull the net in with the catch.

Ox-hide canopy

Steering oar

Steersman

Owner of the boat

DHOW
In the 19th century dhows were as common on the Nile as their papyrus ancestors.

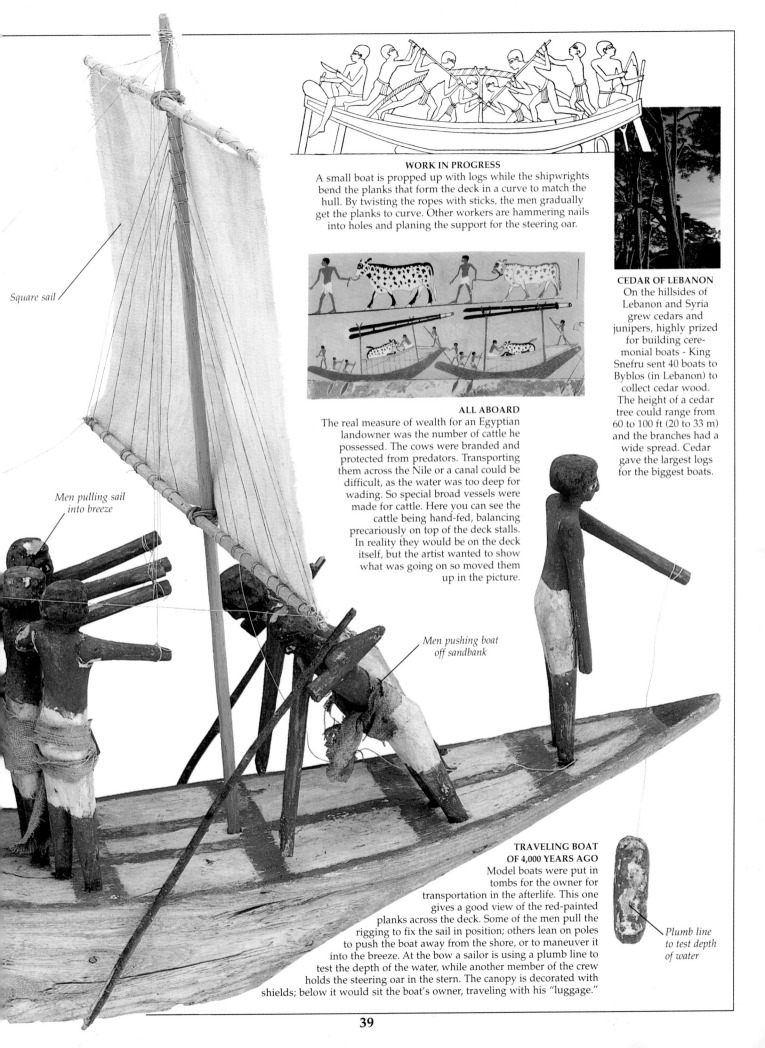

WORK IN PROGRESS

A small boat is propped up with logs while the shipwrights bend the planks that form the deck in a curve to match the hull. By twisting the ropes with sticks, the men gradually get the planks to curve. Other workers are hammering nails into holes and planing the support for the steering oar.

CEDAR OF LEBANON

On the hillsides of Lebanon and Syria grew cedars and junipers, highly prized for building ceremonial boats - King Snefru sent 40 boats to Byblos (in Lebanon) to collect cedar wood. The height of a cedar tree could range from 60 to 100 ft (20 to 33 m) and the branches had a wide spread. Cedar gave the largest logs for the biggest boats.

Square sail

ALL ABOARD

The real measure of wealth for an Egyptian landowner was the number of cattle he possessed. The cows were branded and protected from predators. Transporting them across the Nile or a canal could be difficult, as the water was too deep for wading. So special broad vessels were made for cattle. Here you can see the cattle being hand-fed, balancing precariously on top of the deck stalls. In reality they would be on the deck itself, but the artist wanted to show what was going on so moved them up in the picture.

Men pulling sail into breeze

Men pushing boat off sandbank

TRAVELING BOAT OF 4,000 YEARS AGO

Model boats were put in tombs for the owner for transportation in the afterlife. This one gives a good view of the red-painted planks across the deck. Some of the men pull the rigging to fix the sail in position; others lean on poles to push the boat away from the shore, or to maneuver it into the breeze. At the bow a sailor is using a plumb line to test the depth of the water, while another member of the crew holds the steering oar in the stern. The canopy is decorated with shields; below it would sit the boat's owner, traveling with his "luggage."

Plumb line to test depth of water

Buying and selling

EGYPT WAS THE WEALTHIEST COUNTRY of the ancient world. Some of the gold from the mines of the eastern desert and Nubia was sent abroad in the form of gifts to foreign rulers like the king of Babylon. Manufactured goods and even princesses were sent in exchange to the pharaoh. Although the pharaohs at times controlled long stretches of the Nile beyond the southern frontier at Aswan, produce from deep equatorial Africa was obtained through trade with the princes of Nubia, the area south of the first cataract (rapids) of the Nile. One exchange post was at Kerma, near the third cataract of the Nile. Egyptian merchants brought back a variety of goods like panther skins, greyhounds, giraffe tails for fly whisks, elephant tusks, and animals such as lions and baboons for the temples or palace.

BARTERING
This was a common way of exchanging goods. You might exchange a pair of sandals for a fine walking stick, or a linen garment for a large quantity of food. These men are carrying exchangeable items such as ducks and a jar of wine in a rope basket.

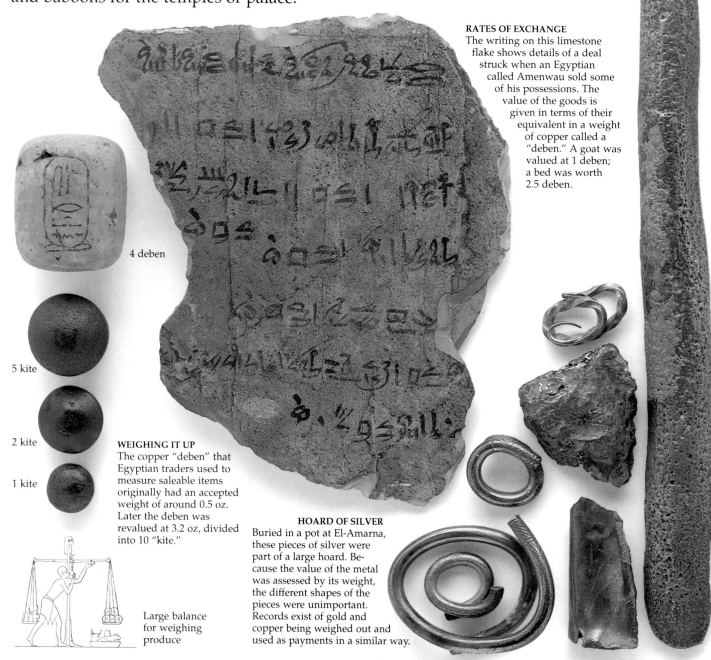

RATES OF EXCHANGE
The writing on this limestone flake shows details of a deal struck when an Egyptian called Amenwau sold some of his possessions. The value of the goods is given in terms of their equivalent in a weight of copper called a "deben." A goat was valued at 1 deben; a bed was worth 2.5 deben.

4 deben

5 kite

2 kite

1 kite

WEIGHING IT UP
The copper "deben" that Egyptian traders used to measure saleable items originally had an accepted weight of around 0.5 oz. Later the deben was revalued at 3.2 oz, divided into 10 "kite."

HOARD OF SILVER
Buried in a pot at El-Amarna, these pieces of silver were part of a large hoard. Because the value of the metal was assessed by its weight, the different shapes of the pieces were unimportant. Records exist of gold and copper being weighed out and used as payments in a similar way.

Large balance for weighing produce

Unloading pottery wine jars from a Nile boat belonging to a high official

IVORY DISH
Elephant tusks came to Egypt via trade with Nubia and were carved into luxury items like this cosmetic spoon. If the supply of ivory from Nubia fell short, the teeth of hippos could be used instead. The design of this cosmetic spoon includes the head of Hathor, goddess of beauty and foreign countries.

Ivory fittings

Ebony handle

Hathor has the ears of the cow, her sacred animal

CASSIA
Cassia, the dried bark of a type of laurel tree, was brought from India. The Egyptians used it for perfume and incense.

The land of Punt

The Egyptians thought of the land of Punt as a remote and exotic place. We do not know exactly where it was, but the most frequent route to it seems to have been along the coast of the Red Sea and then inland toward the Atbara River, a tributary of the Nile. In the 15th century B.C., Queen Hatshepsut sent five boats to Punt. Eventually the boats pulled in at a port on the coast of eastern Sudan. From there the queen's representatives were taken some way inland, where they saw people who lived in houses on stilts to protect them from wild animals. Incense was the main cargo they brought back.

FRANKINCENSE
In Sudan, Ethiopia, Somalia, and Yemen grew trees that yielded frankincense, a fragrant gum resin.

GIFTS FROM SYRIA
These Syrian princes are bringing tribute to the pharaoh. They offer gold vases decorated with lotus flowers, and perfume containers in gold, lapis lazuli, or ivory. One Syrian prince brings his daughter to be raised at court.

FLY WHISK
Ebony, used in this fly whisk, was a highly valued import from central Africa. It was bought with shipments of logs from the Nubians. Courtiers used to carry fly whisks, and these became signs of their status.

Lapis lazuli bull set in gold

LAPIS LAZULI
Merchants from Afghanistan brought this valuable stone to trading centers like Byblos in Lebanon. The Egyptians prized this gem, and thought that the hair of the sun god was made of lapis lazuli.

Unworked lapis lazuli

THE INCENSE TRADE
The myrrh and frankincense carried back from Punt probably originated even farther south. The Egyptians brought back not only the gum resin for incense but also whole trees to plant in front of the queen's temple.

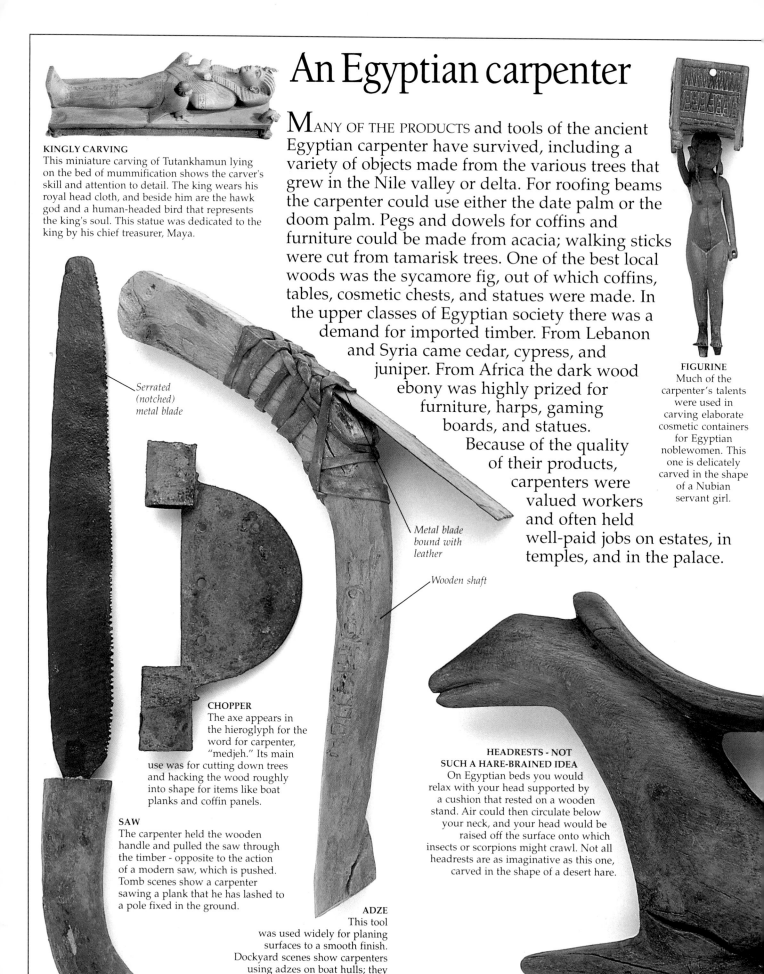

An Egyptian carpenter

KINGLY CARVING
This miniature carving of Tutankhamun lying on the bed of mummification shows the carver's skill and attention to detail. The king wears his royal head cloth, and beside him are the hawk god and a human-headed bird that represents the king's soul. This statue was dedicated to the king by his chief treasurer, Maya.

MANY OF THE PRODUCTS and tools of the ancient Egyptian carpenter have survived, including a variety of objects made from the various trees that grew in the Nile valley or delta. For roofing beams the carpenter could use either the date palm or the doom palm. Pegs and dowels for coffins and furniture could be made from acacia; walking sticks were cut from tamarisk trees. One of the best local woods was the sycamore fig, out of which coffins, tables, cosmetic chests, and statues were made. In the upper classes of Egyptian society there was a demand for imported timber. From Lebanon and Syria came cedar, cypress, and juniper. From Africa the dark wood ebony was highly prized for furniture, harps, gaming boards, and statues.

Because of the quality of their products, carpenters were valued workers and often held well-paid jobs on estates, in temples, and in the palace.

FIGURINE
Much of the carpenter's talents were used in carving elaborate cosmetic containers for Egyptian noblewomen. This one is delicately carved in the shape of a Nubian servant girl.

Serrated (notched) metal blade

Metal blade bound with leather

Wooden shaft

CHOPPER
The axe appears in the hieroglyph for the word for carpenter, "medjeh." Its main use was for cutting down trees and hacking the wood roughly into shape for items like boat planks and coffin panels.

SAW
The carpenter held the wooden handle and pulled the saw through the timber - opposite to the action of a modern saw, which is pushed. Tomb scenes show a carpenter sawing a plank that he has lashed to a pole fixed in the ground.

HEADRESTS - NOT SUCH A HARE-BRAINED IDEA
On Egyptian beds you would relax with your head supported by a cushion that rested on a wooden stand. Air could then circulate below your neck, and your head would be raised off the surface onto which insects or scorpions might crawl. Not all headrests are as imaginative as this one, carved in the shape of a desert hare.

ADZE
This tool was used widely for planing surfaces to a smooth finish. Dockyard scenes show carpenters using adzes on boat hulls; they were also used to carve large funerary chests.

GOAT'S HEAD
Chairs, boxes, and chests were often decorated with animal features. A chair could have legs shaped like lion's paws; a throne could have arms topped by winged snakes or vultures. This small fragment has been exquisitely carved to show the horn, curly fleece, and beard of a goat. It probably came from the decoration of a chest.

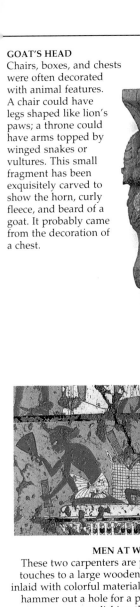

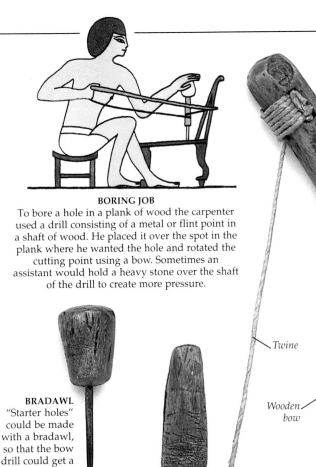

BORING JOB
To bore a hole in a plank of wood the carpenter used a drill consisting of a metal or flint point in a shaft of wood. He placed it over the spot in the plank where he wanted the hole and rotated the cutting point using a bow. Sometimes an assistant would hold a heavy stone over the shaft of the drill to create more pressure.

Twine

Wooden bow

MEN AT WORK
These two carpenters are putting the finishing touches to a large wooden casket that has been inlaid with colorful materials. One uses a mallet to hammer out a hole for a peg while the other is polishing the lid.

BRADAWL
"Starter holes" could be made with a bradawl, so that the bow drill could get a grip. Bradawls were also used by shipwrights to mark the points on planks where wooden pegs were to be fitted.

CHISEL
A carpenter would need a chisel like this for intricate carving and for cutting hieroglyphs into the surfaces of large rectangular wooden coffins.

Hare's ears support pillow and head

Metal drill bit

SMOOTHING STONE
The rough surfaces left after carving could be smoothed down using a stone. The highly polished finish of furniture was often achieved in this way.

DRILL
Carpenters often used a bow drill to make holes for pegs to join pieces of timber together. The wooden shaft of this bow drill is well worn - it was obviously much used by its original owner.

Hunting, fishing, and fowling

AT THE TIME of the pharaohs farming produced an abundance of food, so hunting was mainly a recreation for kings and courtiers. In the Egyptian deserts they hunted wild bulls, gazelles, oryx, antelopes, and lions. King Amenhotep III was proud of killing over 100 fierce lions in ten years; he also killed over 90 wild bulls on one hunting expedition. Often there was no danger to the monarch at all if he went hunting - the bulls would be herded into an enclosure in the marshes and picked off one by one by the pharaoh in his chariot. In the beginning, the courtiers hunted on foot, their followers fencing off areas to hem the animals in; later the courtiers too used chariots. The Nile was also plentiful in fish, which could be caught with hooks or nets. The papyrus thickets sheltered a variety of birds and geese. Here the technique was to hurl a throw stick as the wildfowl flew up from the thickets.

FAMILY OUTING
This nobleman is hunting birds in the papyrus marshes. He is using a snake-shaped throw stick, and the three herons he holds disguise his approach. He has brought his cat, which has caught three birds. With him are his daughter, sitting in the boat, and his elegant wife - who is hardly dressed for the hunt!

ARROWS
Bows and arrows appear on some of the earliest sculptures from ancient Egypt. The arrows were made of reeds and tipped with ivory, bone, flint, or metal.

Flat tips to weaken animal by piercing hide

Sharp tip to kill outright

Cleft end for bowstring

HUNTING THE HIPPO
This animal could cause havoc among reed boats on the Nile and to crops on land. So teams of men in papyrus boats would hunt the hippo, gradually weakening it by repeated spearing until it collapsed. They also used lassoes to hamper the creature's movements.

THROW STICK
Made of wood and shaped like boomerangs, throw sticks were hurled at wildfowl in the hope of stunning them or breaking their neck or a wing.

SPOILS OF THE DESERT
Desert hares are often shown in Egyptian hunting scenes. Sometimes a hare pierced with an arrow will still be trying to scramble to safety. Antelopes and gazelles were also found in the desert, and ostrich eggs were a desert delicacy.

HOOKS
Copper or bronze hooks were used for fishing. The fish were pulled from the water, then gutted and dried in the sun.

WEIGHING THEM DOWN
Like fishermen today, the Egyptians used lead weights to keep their fishing nets under the water.

FISHING NET
This net was used by an Egyptian fisherman about 3,000 years ago. Nets like this made from reed and papyrus twine, were used for trapping both birds and fish. Reed floats kept them in position until they were hauled in by the fisherman.

Courtiers used this type of harpoon to test their skill

Prong to attach rope

HARPOONS
Attached to reed or wooden shafts, metal harpoons were used to catch large game and fish. Symbolically a harpoon was held by kings in the ritual of spearing the hippopotamus of the god Seth. In reality one harpoon would not kill such a large creature; a series of harpoons was required.

The Egyptians at home

HOUSES IN ANCIENT EGYPT were built from bricks made from the Nile mud. The mud was collected in leather buckets and taken to the building site. Here workers added straw and pebbles to the mud to strengthen it, then poured the mixture into wooden frames to make bricks. The bricks were left out in the sun to dry. After the house was built, its walls were covered with plaster, and the inside was often painted - either with patterns or scenes from nature. Inside, the houses were cool, as the small windows let in only a little light. Wealthy families had large houses. Beyond the hall were bedrooms, private apartments, and stairs to the roof. The kitchen was some way from the living rooms, to keep smells away. The ancient Egyptians held parties in their homes, which the children enjoyed as much as their parents.

AROUND THE POOL
A pool was often the central feature of a wealthy family's garden. It was stocked with lotuses and fish, and the water was renewed regularly to keep it fresh. Poolside borders were planted with shrubs and trees such as sycamore figs, date palms, and acacia trees.

HOME COMFORTS
This is a typical home belonging to a successful official, the royal scribe Nakht. The walls were made of mud bricks and coated with limestone plaster. Grille windows high on the walls let in only a little sunlight and dust, and vents trapped the cool north wind. In front was a garden with a pool and trees, in which Nakht and his wife could relax.

SOUL HOUSE
This model shows the house of a poorer family. The model would have been placed in the tomb of the owner, for use in the next life, so it is known as a "soul house." The entrance is through a low arched doorway. A window lets in a little light, and a stairway leads to the roof, where a vent could catch the cool north breeze that the Egyptians loved so much. Food is stored around the walled north courtyard of the house.

Empty vessels

A variety of cups, jars, and pots has survived from ancient Egypt. Among the earliest were stoneware vessels, some made over 5,000 years ago, before the first pharaohs ruled Egypt. These were often superbly crafted from attractive mottled stone. Later, a widely used material was faience, made by heating powdered quartz in a mold. Many different designs were made, including drinking cups and storage containers for wine; some of the jars had pointed bases, showing that they would have been set on stands.

Roof terrace

Offerings for the deceased

WINE JAR
This container for wine is made of faience. Manufactured c. 1000 B.C., it is decorated with diamond and leaf patterns. Vessels like this were often used in wealthy Egyptian homes.

DRINKING CUP
Water, wine, or beer could have been drunk from this beautiful faience cup decorated with a lotus-flower pattern. Its broad base meant that the drinker could easily stand the cup on a convenient table or mat.

BIRD IN HAND
Carved over 5,000 years ago, this vase is a container for oil or other liquids. The contents could be poured in and out through the hole above the wings. It is made of a mottled stone called breccia.

FRUIT BASKET
Baskets were easy to make from either palm leaves or strips of papyrus. Some were patterned with abstract designs or pictures of people. They were often used as household containers - this one holds two doom palm fruits.

FANNING THE FIRE
This household servant is squatting near some charcoal, which he is fanning to make a fire. As well as heat for cooking, the fire provided a focal point for servants to gather around and talk.

This side view shows the graceful carved profiles of some typical Egyptian chairs

Food and drink

THE FERTILE MUD deposited by the annual Nile flood allowed farmers to grow barley and emmer wheat, the mainstay of the Egyptian diet. Stored in granaries, these crops were eventually turned into bread or beer. Egyptian farmers grew vegetables such as onions, garlic, leeks, beans, lentils, and lettuce. There were also gourds, dates and figs, cucumbers and melons, but no citrus fruits. Egyptian bakers made cakes of many shapes and sizes, sweetened by dates or by honey gathered from conical pottery beehives. Grapes grown in the Nile delta or oases of the western desert were plucked for wine-making or drying into raisins. Poorer people would have less meat and poultry, and more fish. The spread at banquets was extremely varied - from ducks, geese, and oxen to oryx and gazelles. There were also pigs, sheep, and goats, which could be boiled or roasted.

BUTCHERS AT WORK
An ox was slaughtered by tying three of its feet together, pushing it on its side, and cutting its throat. The free leg was cut and sometimes given as a religious offering.

IN THE VINEYARD
Two men pluck bunches of grapes from the vines. This job was often given to foreign settlers or prisoners from the Middle East or Nubia. The grapes would then be taken to be crushed by treading.

BREAD
More than 3,000 years old, this bread was baked from barley dough. Its texture was tough: flour often contained grit that got in during grinding. Studies of mummies have shown how coarse bread made Egyptians' teeth wear away.

STRAINER
This wooden syphon with its perforated mouthpiece was used for making beer taste better. Made from mashed loaves of barley-bread, Egyptian beer was very thick and needed to be strained either through a basket or with a syphon.

Perforations for straining

GRAPES
The Egyptians grew most of their grapes in the north, just as they do today. Both red and green grapes provided the fermented juice for wine. They also imported wine from Syria and Greece.

A Syrian soldier serving the pharaoh Akhenaten is sitting drinking beer through a syphon

DELICIOUS DATES
Dates were eaten fresh at harvest time in August or were dried or conserved in a sweet mash. Date wine was also made from both the fruit and the tree's sap.

BABOON WHO DOES NOT GIVE A FIG!
The fruit of the sycamore fig was held in high esteem in ancient Egypt. The modern examples are easily identifiable as the same as those on this sketch. Baboons loved figs and are often shown helping themselves from bowls or straight from the trees.

Modern fig

PALM-TREE FRUIT
These doom-palm fruits come from a 3,000-year-old tomb offering. The fruit has a gingery taste. The outer case of the nut is so tough it could be used as the top end of a drill handle.

Large pomegranate produced by modern agriculture

EGYPTIAN BANQUET
Scribes and nobles were able to enjoy a wide variety of meat, poultry, and fruits. This rich and colorful display of food and drink is from a party scene at a Theban banquet. Wine jars are fixed with their pointed bases in racks and garlanded with leaves. The courses included cakes, baskets of figs and bunches of grapes, the head of a calf, the heart and foreleg of an ox, a plucked goose, and a twist of onions.

POMEGRANATES
The pomegranate was introduced to Egypt from the Middle East and its fruit was soon popular. This dish contains pomegranates that were originally part of a tomb offering. The shape of the fruit was used as a model for jewelry and drinking cups. The skin may have been used to produce a yellowish dye.

Ancient fruits

Song and dance

THE EGYPTIANS ENJOYED LIFE to its fullest. Party scenes on tomb walls, songs on papyri, and musical instruments show us how much music and revelry meant to them. They had great public festivals, at which much wine was drunk and thousands of people were entertained with singing and music from flutes, harps, and castanets. Music was also performed on everyday occasions. Vintners pressed grapes for wine while men clapped rhythm sticks together; farm workers sang to their oxen as the oxen threshed the corn with their hooves; a princess would play the harp while her husband relaxed on a divan; dancers would turn somersaults alongside every procession. We do not know exactly what Egyptian music sounded like, but a small orchestra at a banquet could have string, wind, and percussion sections, and the music probably had a strong beat.

Twine holds disks together

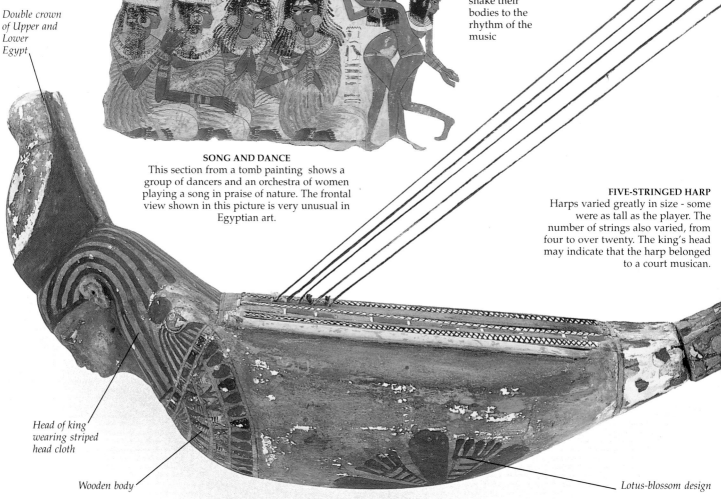

SONG AND DANCE
This section from a tomb painting shows a group of dancers and an orchestra of women playing a song in praise of nature. The frontal view shown in this picture is very unusual in Egyptian art.

Dancing girls shake their bodies to the rhythm of the music

Double crown of Upper and Lower Egypt

FIVE-STRINGED HARP
Harps varied greatly in size - some were as tall as the player. The number of strings also varied, from four to over twenty. The king's head may indicate that the harp belonged to a court musician.

Head of king wearing striped head cloth

Wooden body

Lotus-blossom design

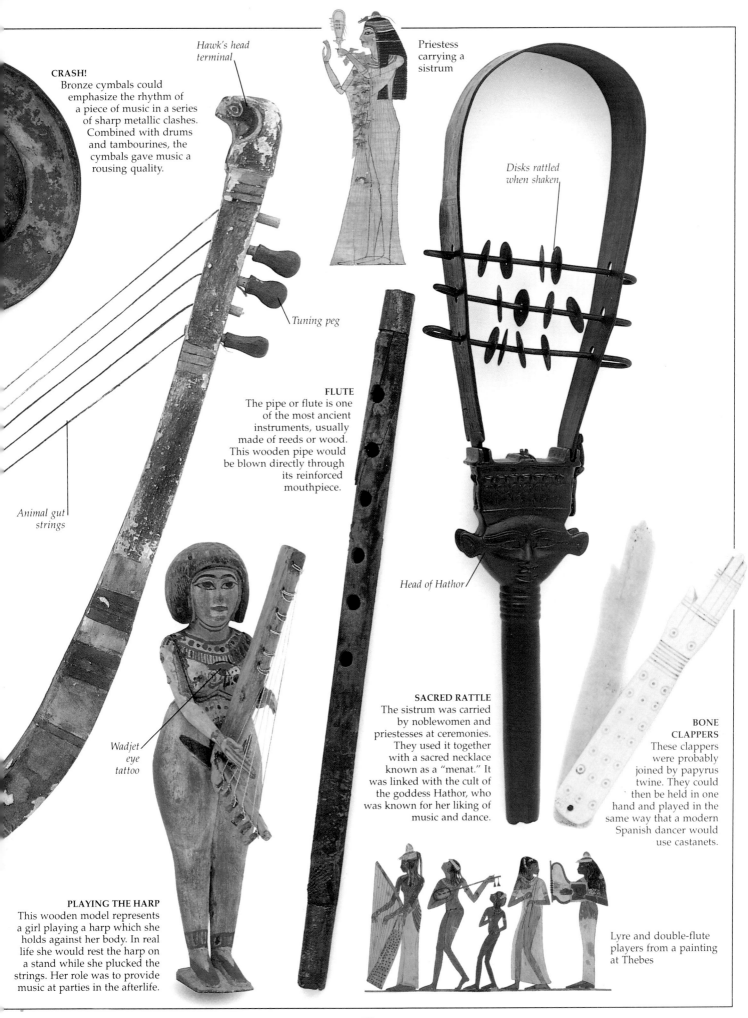

CRASH!
Bronze cymbals could emphasize the rhythm of a piece of music in a series of sharp metallic clashes. Combined with drums and tambourines, the cymbals gave music a rousing quality.

Hawk's head terminal

Priestess carrying a sistrum

Disks rattled when shaken

Tuning peg

Animal gut strings

FLUTE
The pipe or flute is one of the most ancient instruments, usually made of reeds or wood. This wooden pipe would be blown directly through its reinforced mouthpiece.

Head of Hathor

Wadjet eye tattoo

SACRED RATTLE
The sistrum was carried by noblewomen and priestesses at ceremonies. They used it together with a sacred necklace known as a "menat." It was linked with the cult of the goddess Hathor, who was known for her liking of music and dance.

BONE CLAPPERS
These clappers were probably joined by papyrus twine. They could then be held in one hand and played in the same way that a modern Spanish dancer would use castanets.

PLAYING THE HARP
This wooden model represents a girl playing a harp which she holds against her body. In real life she would rest the harp on a stand while she plucked the strings. Her role was to provide music at parties in the afterlife.

Lyre and double-flute players from a painting at Thebes

Toys and games

GAME PIECE
This carved lion's head could have been used as a counter in a number of games.

EVEN AS CHILDREN, the ancient Egyptians enjoyed life. Some of the games they played are still loved by children today, such as "khuzza lawizza," or leapfrog, and tug-of-war. There are also Egyptian paintings showing boys playing soldiers and girls holding hands in a sort of spinning dance. Then there were board games, like snake and the more complicated senet, and a number of toys, including balls, dolls, and toy animals. The Egyptians were also great storytellers, and kept their children amused with popular tales of imagination and enchantment. In one example, a magical wax toy crocodile turns into a real one when thrown into the water - a relevant story for people who lived under the threat of being eaten by crocodiles every day of their lives.

BALLS OR RATTLES?
These colorful balls are made of clay. They were originally filled with seeds or small beads of clay, so that they rattled as they were thrown.

DOLL OR GIRLFRIEND?
The Egyptians made dolls out of wood, with hair of clay beads attached to lengths of twine. Dolls like this one may have been for children, or they may have been made to put in someone's tomb, to act as a companion in the afterlife.

BALL GAMES
A popular pastime, especially for girls, was throwing and catching balls. Ball games were played while standing, or on piggy-back or leaping high into the air.

HORSE ON WHEELS
The Egyptians used horses on hunting trips and to pull their chariots and also on hunting trips. Horseback riding became a favorite pastime of the pharaohs. This toy horse, dating from Roman Egypt, has a saddle mat thrown over it. It was pulled along by a rope through the muzzle.

String to move lower jaw

TOY MOUSE
This wooden mouse had a string fitted to it, which a child could pull to make the tail go up and down.

ROAR OR MEOW?
This roughly carved wooden toy does not seem to know whether it is a cat or a lion. Its main attraction is its movable lower jaw, attached to some string.

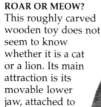

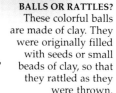

The game of senet

The board game senet symbolized a struggle against the forces of evil that tried to prevent you from reaching the kingdom of the god Osiris. Images on each of the thirty squares of the board stood for advantages like "beauty" or "power," or for perils, like the spearing of a hippo. There were two sets of counters, and moves were made according to the way throw sticks landed.

SPINNING TOPS
A vigorous twist of the fingers or a tug on some papyrus twine wound around the cone would set these tops spinning. They were made of powdered quartz formed in a mold and then glazed. Toys of cheap materials like this meant that even the poorest families could give their children a few amusing games.

YOUR MOVE
This papyrus from the Book of the Dead of the scribe Ani shows Ani and his wife Tutu playing senet. In spite of the fact that the artist has drawn Tutu sitting behind her husband in a rather formal pose, both seem to be enjoying their game.

FIT FOR A KING
Tutankhamun was buried with four senet boards, of which this ebony and ivory board is the finest. It is fitted with a drawer for the counters and fixed on legs that have been delicately carved in the shape of bulls' feet.

Hieroglyph of pharaoh's name

Stone counter used in the snake game

THE GAME OF SNAKE
One of the earliest board games discovered in Egypt was called "snake" because the stone board represented a serpent coiled with its head in the center. The winner was the first to move his or her counter around the squares on the snake's body to the center. The stone counters are sometimes carved with the names of some of Egypt's earliest pharaohs.

From fabric to finery

LINEN, made from flax (plant fiber) provided clothing materials for everyone in ancient Egypt. The earliest picture of a loom in Egypt is on a pottery bowl dated to c. 3000 B.C. and flax was used for thousands of years after that. A pharaoh would have exceptionally fine linen; workers wore loincloths of coarser fabric. The Egyptians had clever ways of reducing wear on linen clothes - soldiers would cover the rear of their kilts with leather netting; domestic servants wore nets of cheap but colorful beads over their dresses. The basic courtier's kilt consisted of a linen cloth wrapped around the waist and secured by a knot, often elaborately tied. Cloaks gradually developed for use as overgarments. Women wore long, close-fitting dresses, often with beautifully pleated cloaks. There are still only vague ideas about how the Egyptians put pleats into their clothes - perhaps they used a board with a grooved surface. The number of pleats is probably exaggerated in many statues. The Egyptians learned the art of dyeing their clothes in colorful patterns from the Middle East, but the technique was never widespread.

MAN AND WIFE
This worker wears a pleated calf-length kilt; his wife wears a cloak. Their finely braided wigs have perfume pomades (p. 58).

LEATHER SANDALS
These sandals are made from strips of ox leather stitched together with papyrus twine. Leather is an unusual material for Egyptian footwear.

Reinforced edge

REED SANDALS
Papyrus and other reeds, in plentiful supply, were the most common materials for sandals. Reed sandals were worn at all levels of society; priests were forbidden to wear any other material on their feet.

Twine securing strap

WIGS
These courtiers on a wall relief at Memphis are wearing typical wigs and costumes with billowing sleeves. The wigs were made of human hair kept in place with beeswax.

PRINCESS OR QUEEN?
This statue is one of many intriguing works of art that survive from the reign of Akhenaten (p. 10). It represents Akhenaten's queen, Nefertiti, or one of her daughters. She is shown wearing a very fine garment of royal linen. The dress would have had many pleats, but probably not as many as shown by the sculptor.

IN THE GROOVE
This grooved board may have been used for pleating. The damp garment would be pressed into the grooves.

FLAX COMB
The first stage in making linen was to remove the flax heads with a long comb like this one. Then the flax stems were soaked and beaten to separate the fibers from the stalk and combed again to prepare them for spinning.

LINEN SHEET
Types of linen in ancient Egypt ranged from coarse material like this, which most people would have used, to the finest gauze worn by kings and queens.

SPINDLE
The flax fibers were spun on sticks, or spindles, which had a weighted circular whorl on one end. Whorls dating from around 3000 B.C. have been discovered.

SPINNER
This girl is using her left hand to draw out the twisted slivers of fibers (the rove), which are attached to the rotating spindle balanced by the weight of the whorl.

All that glitters

YOU CAN SEE the glint of gold everywhere in Egyptian jewelry - mines between the Nile and the Red Sea coast yielded large quantities of this precious metal. The gold could be beaten into shape or cast in molds. Goldsmiths also made patterns using a method called granulation, in which tiny grains of gold were attached to an object by soldering. Egyptian jewelers had access to many semiprecious stones from the deserts - orange-red carnelian, green feldspar, and mauve amethyst. They also imported stones. From mines in the Sinai peninsula came light blue turquoise and trade routes from Afghanistan brought rich blue lapis lazuli to Egypt. But Egyptian jewelers had no knowledge of precious stones like diamonds, emeralds, and rubies.

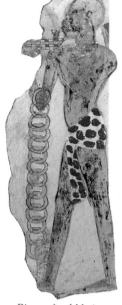

Rings of gold being brought to Egypt from Nubia

ROYAL BRACELET
This bracelet, made for Prince Nemareth, has a central design showing the god Horus as a child (p. 27). He is sitting on a lotus and is protected by cobras. Like many children in Egyptian art, he is portrayed sucking his finger.

Hieroglyphs give name of owner

Cowrie shell shows desire of wearer to have children

LUCKY BELT
This is the surviving section of a belt. In addition to cowrie shells made of electrum (a mixture of gold and silver), the belt contains beads of carnelian, amethyst, lapis lazuli, and turquoise.

A STAR IS BORN
This gold star was worn on the fore-head as a diadem. It dates from the Roman period of Egypt. The Roman mummy mask shows a priest wearing a diadem.

Gold diadem

EAR ORNAMENTS
Middle Eastern influence led the Egyptians to have their ear lobes pierced and wear earrings. These earrings show how large the holes had to be to fit these studs of the 14th century B.C.

Gold earrings

Faience stud

Glass stud

Jasper stud

FALCON PECTORAL
This falcon was worn on the chest. It represents the god Re-Harakhty. The metal originally formed a framework for segments of faience, glass, or gems. This technique is called cloisonné work. Only traces of the inlay now remain.

Traces of original inlay

Metal strips bent into shape and soldered onto base

Talon holds the "shenu" symbol, meaning eternity

JEWELERS AT WORK
Many metal objects were made by casting - heating the metal until it was liquid (top) and then pouring it into molds (above) in the shapes of the objects required.

GIFT OF A KING
Outstanding service to the state was rewarded by a gift of jewelry from the king. He would lean out of a window and drop bracelets or collars to the nobles waiting respectfully below. This collar of honor has three rows of gold rings threaded tightly together on twine. It was tied in position at the back of the neck. Sometimes the pharaohs themselves wore collars like this.

FINGER RINGS
Rings often incorporated a swiveling stone in the shape of a scarab beetle (p. 24). The underside was carved with a name or good-luck design. These scarabs are made of steatite (soapstone), an easy material to carve.

Fish amulets, to prevent drowning

Scarab

Steatite and gold ring

Steatite and gold ring

Silver ring

This figure is wearing its hair in a sidelock, to represent youth.

Beards or sidelocks of youth

Heh, god of "millions of years," symbolizes long life

57

Adorning the body

THE EGYPTIANS were lovers of beauty and fashion. Many of their personal names are based on the word "nefer," meaning "beautiful" - for example, Nefret, Nefertiti, and Nefertari. The goddess associated with adornment was "Hathor the Golden," who is seen as the ideal of beauty in love poetry of the time. Egyptian men and women used eye paint, which was made from minerals ground on fine slate palettes. They went to great lengths in adorning themselves with cosmetics, wigs, floral garlands, and fine linen. Many objects like combs and mirrors have survived and show how important personal appearance was to the Egyptians. "Put myrrh on your head and dress up in beautiful clothes" says one song.

Malachite

Tube with royal inscription

APPLICATORS
These were used for scooping, mixing, and applying pigment.

CRAFTSMAN'S MASTERPIECE
The mother duck's back wings slide across to give access to the face cream inside.

CONTAINERS
Ground mineral for eye paint was mixed with water and kept in tubes like these. The one with the royal inscription may have been a gift to a courtier.

PERFUME POMADES
Courtiers tied cones of scented animal fat to their wigs, sometimes with a lotus blossom. The fat would melt and slide down the wig.

Pot made of the rare stone anhydrite

MIRROR
Courtiers used polished bronze or copper mirrors. Here a naked servant girl holding a bird forms the handle, suggesting love and beauty.

Galena

Polished metal reflective surface

Iron oxide

BATH AND MASSAGE
This noblewoman kneels on a mat while a friend holds a flower for her to smell. Her bath is symbolized by water being scattered over her; she is also being given a shoulder massage.

Tweezers

PIGMENTS
From malachite, a copper ore, the Egyptians produced green eye paint to symbolize fertility. The lead ore known as galena gave a gray-black eye paint (today often called kohl). Cheeks could be rouged and lips painted red by using ochers made of oxides of iron which are plentiful throughout Egypt. Some fat would probably be mixed with the makeup when it was applied to the face.

PLUCKING AND CURLING
Priests and women used tweezers to remove hair. Women also curled their hair with tongs.

Hair curler

Double ends for different-size curls

CLOSE SHAVE
Bronze or copper razors were probably as uncomfortable to use as they look, unless in the hands of the professional traveling barbers of ancient Egypt.

FLORAL SPOON
The handle of this container represents a bunch of flowers tied together; the buds are made of pink-stained ivory. The top swivels to reveal or cover the cosmetic.

WOODEN COMB
Most Egyptians did not have long hair, but their wigs could be quite long and heavy, sometimes with three different layers of curls and fringes, so ivory and wooden combs were a necessity.

TOUCHING UP
A noblewoman called Ipwet appears in this relief. She holds a mirror while she dabs powder onto her cheeks.

HAIRPINS
These were used to keep elaborate curls in position or hold perfumed pomades in place on wigs.

Animals of the Nile valley

THE ANCIENT EGYPTIANS shared their environment with many different beasts, birds, reptiles, and fish. Out in the desert east and west of the Nile valley you would find ferocious lions and wild bulls as well as timid antelopes and gazelles. These animals either hunted their prey or grazed on the borders of the flood plain. The stillness of night would suddenly be broken by the eerie howls of scavenging hyenas and jackals fighting over carcasses. In the papyrus thickets beside the Nile there would be nests of birds like pintail ducks, cormorants, pelicans, and hoopoes. Lurking on the river banks would be crocodiles, and in the water you might see hippos with Nile perch and catfish darting around them. Animals appear on many ancient Egyptian objects. They were thought of as part of the "world system" made by the sun god, and as the earthly versions of many gods. Animal symbols were also used in hieroglyphics.

LION
The lion represented strength and domination, and so became an emblem of the god-king himself. Rarely is the lion shown being hunted by any other person than the pharaoh. This gold lion was originally part of a necklace.

PEEK-A-BOO
The goddess Hathor was often portrayed as a cow in the papyrus marshes.

ANIMAL ANTICS
Satirical papyri show the topsy-turvy Egyptian sense of humor. On this example, two enemies, the antelope and the lion, are enjoying a friendly game of senet (p. 53). A jackal playing a double flute escorts a herd of goats while a cat lovingly attends to some geese. The lion at the right end seems to be amused by the antics of an ox on a couch.

WILD SHEEP AND NONCHALANT CAT
On this cosmetic container a wild sheep, or mouflon, is stepping carefully over a crouching cat that is clearly determined not to move. Rams symbolized some of the most important gods in ancient Egypt. A curly-horned ram could represent Amun-Re, king of the gods.

Crown of Osiris, made of ram's horns, reeds, and ostrich feathers

CROCODILE GOD
The peril of being snatched and eaten by crocodiles led the Egyptians to try to get these dangerous creatures on their side. Consequently the crocodile became the symbol of the god Sobek, and priests used to decorate sacred crocodiles with jewelry and mummify them when they died.

HIPPOS
Nothing illustrates the Egyptian fondness for visual humor quite as well as their models of standing hippos. The male hippo was a creature of evil omen because of its association with the god Seth, arch-enemy of Osiris and Horus, rightful rulers of Egypt. In reality, hippos could easily overturn a papyrus boat, and were often hunted for this reason.

FISH FLASK
This glass fish was made by molding the glass over a core. The ripples are meant to indicate the fish's scales. The flask was designed to hold perfume, which could be poured out of the mouth into the owner's hand. Objects like this show the beauty of the fishes of the Nile and the Red Sea.

GEESE ON PARADE
These geese are part of a very early tomb painting and were meant to ensure that the supply of food in the afterlife would not run out.

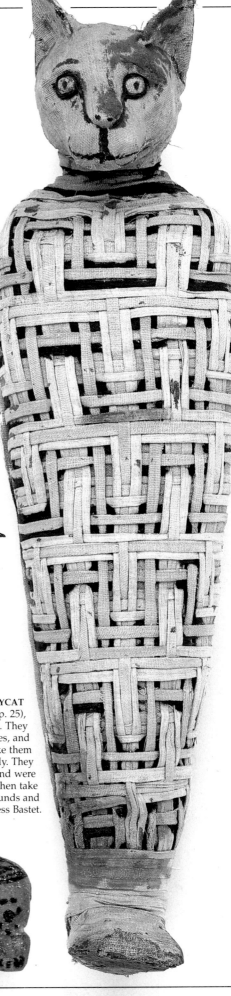

PUZZLED PUSSYCAT
Cats, sacred to the goddess Bastet (p. 25), were mummified when they died. They were wrapped in linen bandages, and their faces were painted to make them look bewildered - or just plain silly. They were put in cat-shaped coffins and were sold to temple visitors, who could then take them to the temple burial grounds and dedicate them to the goddess Bastet.

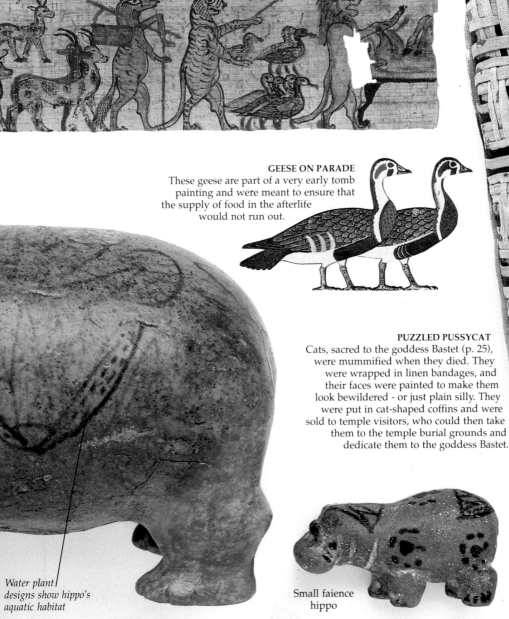

Water plant designs show hippo's aquatic habitat

Small faience hippo

Egypt after the pharaohs

EGYPT WAS INVADED by foreigners several times in the last 1,000 years B.C. The invaders included the Sudanese, the Persians, and the Macedonians under Alexander the Great. Alexander was followed by his general Ptolemy, who founded a dynasty that ruled from Alexandria. These rulers spoke Greek and worshiped Greek gods and goddesses, but on temple walls they were portrayed as traditional Egyptian rulers. In 30 B.C. Egypt passed into Roman hands, and gradually, following the conversion to Christianity of the Roman emperors, churches and monasteries replaced the temples. The Arab invasion of the 7th century A.D. turned Egypt into the mainly Muslim country that it is today.

CLEOPATRA
Queen Cleopatra VII was the last in a line of Greek rulers of Egypt. Her suicide was famous, but there is no historical evidence to back up the familiar story that she died of the bite of a snake called an asp.

The Romans

The Roman world took grain from Egypt's fields and gold from its mines. But although the Romans exploited Egypt, they also built temples. The names of emperors like Augustus and Tiberius were written in hieroglyphs just like those of the pharaohs, and the emperors were sometimes pictured wearing elaborate Egyptian crowns.

EMPEROR AS HORUS
Just as the Egyptian pharaoh was identified with the god Horus (p. 27), so the Roman emperors were sometimes portrayed as this hawk-headed god. The hawk's feathers suggest metal armor, and the figure wears Roman sandals and a toga.

Mummy of Artemidorus

Roman child's mummy

ROMAN MUMMIES
Mummies of the Roman period often had lifelike portraits of the deceased. The coffin above shows its owner, Artemidorus, painted in typical wide-eyed Roman style. The pigment was mixed with beeswax to give bright colors. The idea of these portraits was to help a person's spirit identify the body to which it belonged. They look toward you as if they had been called by name.

The Christians

Egypt officially turned to Christianity with the conversion of the Roman Empire in A.D. 324, although there were Christian hermits living in caves in Egypt before that. The version of Christianity that eventually triumphed in Egypt was called Coptic. It still flourishes in the country today and Coptic monks still live in thriving monasteries. Recently the relics of Saint Mark, who is said to have introduced Christianity into Egypt, were sent back from Venice to Cairo.

SURVIVOR
Qasr Ibrim, a mountain in Nubia, was the center of a Christian diocese that was stormed by Muslim troops. This silver cross was one of the items to survive the attack.

WARRIOR SAINT
The image of the god Horus on horseback spearing his rival Seth was adopted by the early Christians in Egypt to portray warrior saints like St. George and St. Menas.

Tapestry roundel showing the victorious St. George

STREET SCENE
Until the 19th century the streets of Cairo contained stalls - each selling the products of one craft - running alongside the walls, minarets, and domes of the mosques.

Brass openwork design

The Muslims

Arab armies, skilled in warfare on horseback, conquered Egypt in the 7th century A.D. They ruled through the existing, mainly Christian, bureaucracy. But Islam became the state religion, Arabic the official language, and the new city of el-Qahira later became the capital, Cairo. Eventually Egypt was conquered by the Turks, and it was not until the 1960s that the country was again governed by a native Egyptian.

INCENSE BURNER
This vessel, made about 1,000 years ago, was used in a mosque. Burning incense was part of the ritual of purity observed by Muslims, which included removing shoes and washing upon entering a mosque.

Index

Acknowledgments

Dorling Kindersley would like to thank:
The Department of Egyptian Antiquities, British Museum for the provision of artefacts for photography; James Puttnam for his invaluable assistance in arranging for artefacts to be photographed and for his help with picture research; Celia Clear of British Museum Publications; the Departments of Oriental Antiquities and Medieval and Later Antiquities, British Museum for extra objects for photography; Morgan Reid for his advice on photographic lighting; Meryl Silbert for production; Karl Shone for special photography (pp. 20-21); Lester Cheeseman for his desktop publishing expertise.

Picture credits
t=top b=bottom m=middle l=left r=right

Agyptisches Museum/Photo: Staatliche Museen zu Berlin: 48bl
Ancient Art & Architecture Collection: 10bl, 10 bm, 11tr, 11bl, 14tr, 28-9t
Anglo Aquarium Plant Co./Barbara Thomas: 26ml
Bridgeman Art Library: 24tr, 28tl, 28br
British Museum: 6b, 9tr, 10m, 11m, 14br, 15tl, 15tm, 15br, 16tr, 18m, 19t, 19br, 22tl, 26m, 27tl, 27mr, 28m, 29r, 30mr, 32, 33, 34m, 35mr, 40tl, 41t, 41bm, 44m, 45tl, 46l, 46b, 49bl, 50m, 51tm, 53tm, 56tl, 56bl, 57br, 58bm, 59bm, 60tr, 60-1m, 62bl, 62bm, 63tr
Brtitish Museum/Nina M. de Garis Davies: 39m, 48mr, 51b, 61m
Peter Clayton: 26tl, 38m
Bruce Coleman Ltd: 41mr

Michael Dixon, Photo Resources: 10tr, 25tl
Egypt Exploration Society, London: 54br
Mary Evans Picture Library: 57tr, 62tr
Werner Forman Archive: 8tr
Editions Gallimard: 20tl
Griffith Institute, Ashmolean Museum, Oxford: 23b
Robert Harding Picture Library: 12ml, 13bl, 23mr, 24bl, 36-7b, 39tr, 42tl, 53ml, 54tl
George Hart: 23m, 29m
Michael Holford: 41br
Hutchison Library: 9mr
Courtesy of the Oriental Institute of the University of Chicago: 44-5b
Popperfoto: 38tl
James Puttnam: 31ml
Louvre/© Réunion des Musées Nationaux: 55tm

Uni-Dia Verlag: 43 ml
University College, London: 22b, 35ml
Roger Wood: 32tl
Verlag Philipp von Zabern/Cairo Museum: 8-9b

Every effort has been made to trace the copyright holders and we apologize in advance for any unintentional omissions. We would be pleased to insert the appropriate acknowledgment in any subsequent edition of this publication.

Illustrators
Thomas Keenes: 21tl, 32br, 33bl, 43t, 55bc
Eugene Fleury: 8cl

Picture Research Kathy Lockley

1 BIRD

2 ROCKS & MINERALS

3 SKELETON

4 ARMS & ARMOR

5 TREE

6 POND & RIVER

7 BUTTERFLY & MOTH

8 SPORTS

9 SHELL

10 EARLY HUMANS

11 MAMMAL

12 MUSIC

13 DINOSAUR

14 PLANT

15 SEASHORE

16 FLAG

17 INSECT

18 MONEY

19 FOSSIL

20 FISH

21 CAR

22 FLYING MACHINE

23 ANCIENT EGYPT

24 ANCIENT ROME

25 CRYSTAL & GEM

26 REPTILE

27 INVENTION

28 WEATHER

29 CAT

30 BIBLE LANDS

31 EXPLORER

32 DOGS

33 HORSE

34 FILM

35 COSTUME

36 BOAT

37 ANCIENT GREECE

38 VOLCANO & EARTHQUAKE

39 TRAIN

40 SHARK

41 AMPHIBIAN

42 ELEPHANT

43 KNIGHT

44 MUMMY

45 COWBOY

46 WHALE

47 AZTEC, INCA & MAYA

48 BOOK

49 CASTLE

50 VIKING

51 DESERT

52 PREHISTORIC LIFE

53 PYRAMID

54 JUNGLE

55 ANCIENT CHINA

56 ARCHEOLOGY

57 ARCTIC & ANTARCTIC

58 BUILDING

59 PIRATE

60 NORTH AMERICAN INDIAN

61 AFRICA

62 OCEAN

63 BATTLE

64 GORILLA, MONKEY & APE

65 MEDIEVAL LIFE

66 FARM

67 SPY

68 RELIGION

69 EAGLE & BIRDS OF PREY

70 WITCHES & MAGIC-MAKERS

71 SPACE EXPLORATION

72 SHIPWRECK